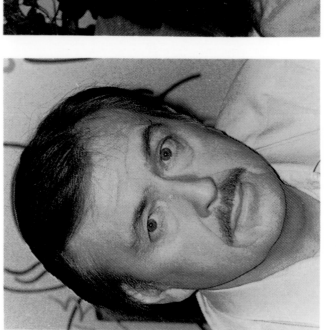

BRAD STEIGER and **SHERRY HANSEN STEIGER**
Authors of *More Strange Powers of Pets*
Published by Donald I. Fine, Inc.
October 11, 1994; 224pp; $18.95

MORE STRANGE POWERS OF PETS

MORE STRANGE POWERS OF PETS

by Brad Steiger
& Sherry Hansen Steiger

DONALD I. FINE, INC.
New York

Library of Congress Catalogue Card Number: 94-071102

ISBN: 1-55611-405-2

Manufactured in the United States of America

10 9 8 7 6 5 4 3 2 1

Designed by Irving Perkins Associates

Dedicated to the elegant souls of the animals of this world and the other

Contents

Part Four
PETS IN THE SPOTLIGHT: THE CELEBRITIES
AND THE INHERITORS   **139**

Part Five
THE RESCUERS AND THE WARRIORS   159

Introduction

Our dear friend the late Fay Clark was known by all of his friends and associates as a person who "had a way with animals." We will always remember the way he would greet our cats and dog upon his arrival in our home, speaking to them and acknowledging their presence just as he would the human members of our family. It was even more interesting to watch the way our "four-legged children" were drawn toward him as if he were a magnet and they were iron filings. And they would listen to his every word, standing motionless before him, gazing up at him as if he brought them personal greetings from the Great Animal Spirit.

At the memorial service that celebrated the life of Fay Marvin Clark on October 23, 1991, Dr. Brent Haskell shared the following experience with those friends and family who had gathered at the First United Methodist Church in Perry, Iowa:

"One of the most beautiful things about Fay was his internal quietness. There was always a sense of great peace that I felt whenever I was around him. Fay had learned at a young age to communicate with nature, including animals.

"One day some friends were visiting and asked him to demonstrate [his ability to communicate with animals]. He walked with them outside to a tree where a mother robin was sitting on her nest. Fay asked the bird if it would be all right with her if he showed his friends the eggs in her nest.

"Fay then walked over to the nest, gently picked up the bird in his hands, showed the eggs to his dumbfounded friends, gently placed the bird back on her nest, thanked her, and left.

"[Dr. Haskell] couldn't refrain from asking Fay, 'How do you do that? What happens between you and the bird?'

"He replied, 'When you completely silence your mind, then there is no fear; and you become one with the bird. It works with all of nature the same way. But if—and this is important—you become aware of yourself as human, as separate from the bird, it will become frightened and fly away.' "

In his youth, Fay had lived for a time among the Winnebago Indian tribe, and it seemed as though he was a most apt student when it came to his perceiving the oneness of all life as taught by the venerable medicine priests. In those few words, he may well have presented us with the essence of how we may better communicate with our pets and with all of nature: Completely silence the mind and become one with all of nature. If you become aware of yourself as human, you will frighten the creature away.

Throughout this book you will read the accounts of ordinary people and their ordinary pets who entered a dimension of time, space and love where the normal limitations of the ordinary world no longer have any meaning. There are no acceptable scientific explanations for most of the experiences recorded in this book. At least not yet there aren't. No one can explain how a lost pet can find its way to its owner's new home in a city and state completely foreign to its ordinary knowledge. No one can explain how a pet can survive incredible feats of endurance in order to better serve its owner. Certainly, the power of love may explain a great deal of the animal's motivation, but even that mighty energy must exist in a medium, a dimension of being, that can somehow circumvent the seemingly impossible barriers of our three-dimensional world of physical reality.

In her paper on personal experiences which she presented at the thirty-sixth annual convention of the Parapsychological Association, August 15–19, 1993, in Toronto, Rhea A. White recalled coming upon a passage regarding animal psychism in Anna Sewell's well-known book, *Black Beauty*, in which the author writes: "God has given . . . animals knowledge which did not depend on reason and which was much more prompt and perfect in its way and by which they had often saved the lives of men."

In this passage, parapsychologist White says that she recognizes her own definition of ESP, which is "the ability to obtain information without using sensory or rational faculties."

The distinguished medical doctor, psychiatrist, and parapsychologist Dr. Berthold Eric Schwarz has long been sensitive to the psychic dimension that exists between humans and their pets. In Vol. 20, No. 2 [1973] of the *Journal of the American Society of Psychosomatic Dentistry and Medicine,* Dr. Schwarz contributed a lengthy article entitled "Possible Human-Animal Paranormal Events," in which he presented numerous illustrations of apparent animal-human ESP.

"Because of the intimate nature of their work, psychiatrists are favorably situated to observe possible telepathy between patients and their pets, as well as to be sensitive to such possibilities in their own lives," Dr. Schwarz writes. "For example, Mrs. Krystal and her sons presented convincing evidence of how, when she was traveling in Mexico, she telepathically (and correctly) learned of her dog's death in Maryland."

After detailing a number of fascinating animal-human telepathic and clairvoyant linkups, Dr. Schwarz concludes his article with several provocative questions: "Are there other dimensions to the life spectrum so that when the man-beast sensitivities are attuned to a common resonance these strange communications can take place? What might be the common physical modalities for such esoteric biocommunications?"

We do not pretend to have the answers to such questions, but this book shall certainly provide enormous amounts of additional data which demonstrate clearly that such a psychic dimension between humans and animals does exist. Perhaps somewhere in these pages are the clues that can solve the age-old riddle of human-animal paranormal events.

Part One

THE MYSTERIOUS PSYCHIC DIMENSION WE SHARE WITH OUR PETS

Incredible Sagas of Pets That Found Their Way Home

In our book *Strange Powers of Pets* (Donald I. Fine hardcover edition, 1992; Berkley mass market edition, 1993), we told of a number of pets who had found their way back home after having been lost—or even more remarkably, found their way to their owners' new homes where they had never been.

Included in our previous collection was a brief account of Bobbie, the present world champion in the mysterious "Lassie Come Home" category of our pets' paranormal prowess. In 1923, Bobbie, a collie, somehow accomplished an extraordinary odyssey of 3,000 miles, from Wolcott, Indiana, where his owner had been visiting relatives, back to their home in Silverton, Oregon. Forever immortalized in Charles Alexander's book *Bobbie: A Great Collie of Oregon,* the collie's journey, managed in six months of steady walking, was nearly equaled by a cat named Tom, who, in 1949, trekked a bit over 2,500 miles, from St. Petersburg, Florida, to San Gabriel, California, to be reunited with owners who had been worried that he couldn't adjust to *driving* such a distance with them in the car.

Tom took a little longer. He needed two years and six weeks to find his owners' new home. We can probably call the score even, though, when we remember that Bobbie was finding his way *back* home, while Tom had to locate a completely new environment in a different state on the opposite coast.

In the same year, 1949, that Tom was hiking from Florida to the new residence in California, a cat named Rusty pulled off one of the most extraordinary returns in the annals of "pet returns" stories and earned a permanent pedestal in the *Strange Powers of Pets* Hall of Fame.*

---

* For information about how you can nominate your pet for inclusion in Sherry and Brad Steiger's *Strange Powers of Pets* Hall of Fame, send a stamped, self-addressed envelope to the authors in care of the publisher.

It seems that Rusty's human family somehow misplaced him while they were visiting Boston. After the usual desperate and tearful search for their missing pet, they gave up the hunt and returned home to Chicago, a thousand miles away.

Eighty-three days later, Rusty was back home, scratching on the door to be let in.

Puzzled experts on such matters were forced to come to the conclusion that the clever cat had managed to hitch an occasional ride on a train or a truck in order to traverse such a distance in so few days.

Okay, so Tom still has the points on Rusty in the "Locating a New Home" category. Rusty was, after all, *returning* home. But how did Rusty know which trains, trucks or automobiles would take him in the direction of Chicago, Illinois, and not New Orleans, Louisiana?

In 1951, a cat named Sugar required fourteen months to find her way back home to Gage, Oklahoma, from Anderson, California, a distance of 1,400 miles.

Howie, a most resilient Persian cat, took twelve months to trek 1,000 miles across the vast and rugged Australian outback in order to return to his home in Adelaide in 1977.

In 1979, a five-year-old Alsatian female named Nick became separated from her owner while on a camping trip in the southern Arizona desert. Four months later, Nick staggered back to her home in Selah, Washington. If one may assume that Nick trod a more or less straight line on those 2,000 miles from Arizona to Washington, then she somehow managed to conquer some of the roughest terrain on earth, terrain that includes the Grand Canyon, a number of icy rivers, and the towering, snow-covered mountains of Nevada and Oregon.

Gyp, a German police dog owned by Herbert Neff of Knoxville, Tennessee, was a most unusual canine who kept running away from home, but who always returned at Christmas. The Neffs simply had to regard him as their Christmas dog, for Gyp came back each successive December 25 for nine years.

*   *   *

In 1986, Sam the Siamese cat moved with his owner Linda Thompson when she decided to leave Beaver Dam, Wisconsin, to test the climate in Tucson, Arizona.

After a year, however, Linda decided that things were pretty good back in Beaver Dam, so she made plans to return home. The problem was that her new landlords in Wisconsin informed her that they absolutely would not accept pets among their boarders.

Sadly, Linda bade her old friend Sam farewell and put him up for adoption with the Humane Society in Tucson before she began the 1,400 mile drive back to Beaver Dam.

Four years later, in 1991, some of Linda's friends from the old neighborhood in Beaver Dam called her at her new place and told her that she had better come and have a look at an ornery cat that was living in a garage near her former home.

Linda was astonished to see that Sam the Siamese had somehow made his way back to Wisconsin. It had taken him four years to hike the 1,400 miles and find the old neighborhood in Beaver Dam.

"It's good to have him back home," she said.

Chinook, a white German shepherd, left Scottsbluff, Nebraska, in 1961 with his owner, Joe Martinez. Somehow, while staying in a Sacramento, California, motel, Martinez and his dog became separated. Although he spent hours searching for Chinook, Martinez was forced to accept the sad fact that his dog had disappeared.

In March 1964, Chinook limped, weary and ragged, into the yard of Martinez's former home in Scottsbluff. It had taken the shepherd three years to accomplish the 1,400-mile odyssey from Sacramento to Scottsbluff.

No one ever got around to tabulating Tam's miles—and he was never really lost—but the dachshund from Tamanraset in the Sahara Desert must have set a record for air miles traveled. For a period of ten years in the late 1950s to early 1960s, Tam traveled constantly from one desert airfield to another. Incredibly, he logged all those miles as a stowaway, never as a passenger, somehow managing to make his way aboard the planes unnoticed.

Lord Trekked 500 Miles to Be Reunited with His Owner

They had met on the beach. He seemed to be down on his luck, half-starved, and in terrible physical condition. His coat was ragged and patches of his skin showed through. When Paquita Soler of Gandia, Spain, perceived the stranger, there was no question that he was in definite need of a friend.

Paquita had not planned on such an encounter during her beach stroll on that day in 1992. At the age of sixty-seven, she really didn't need a new relationship; and she certainly didn't wish to add any new responsibilities to her life pattern.

She walked on, trying to ignore the stranger's plight, attempting to close her heart to the sad eyes, the weak and pathetic whining.

Then she turned and scooped the little puppy into her arms. She could not walk away from a fellow creature's troubles.

The pup appeared to be about six months old. Some thoughtless person had apparently dumped the little guy and left him to his own survival instincts. But scraps of food along the Spanish beach were hard to come by when he had to compete with the endlessly hungry, ceaselessly swooping seagulls. The beach was already supporting its maximum number of scavengers.

Once she managed to get him to her home and set a plate of food before him, Paquita was bemused that he still nibbled at the food with grace and good manners. She knew that he had to be starving and desperate for food, but he conducted himself as though he were being served one of his regular three square meals a day.

Since he behaved as though he were lord of the manor, Paquita decided to name him Lord.

With the help of a local veterinarian, she nursed Lord back to full health; and he became her constant companion. As the months passed, Paquita grew amazed at the depths of devotion that Lord seemed to hold for her.

And then, late in the year, Paquita received notice from her doctor of a rather serious health matter that had to be taken care of as soon as possible. It was advised that she travel to Paris for medical treatment. It was further advised that she allow two months for such treatment to be effective.

More concerned about leaving Lord than the seriousness of her health condition, Paquita spent troubled hours deciding on exactly what would be the best course of action to follow to cause her young dog the least amount of stress.

She presented her problem to some friends who lived in the French town of Montpellier, and they generously offered to board Lord for the two months that she would be receiving the required medical treatment in Paris.

Relieved that Lord would be near to her and would not have to be left in a kennel back in Spain, Paquita delivered him into the care of her friends, admonished the young dog to be on his best behavior, and traveled on to Paris to receive the prescribed treatments with an easy mind.

While the medical therapy was successful, Paquita's tranquil thoughts were demolished when she returned to her friends' home in January 1993 and was sadly informed that Lord had run away. He had been disconsolate and so grieved by her absence that he had left quietly one night and had not been seen for weeks.

Paquita was heartbroken when she learned of Lord's disappearance. He was wandering about in a confused state of mind in south central France, more than 500 miles from their home in Gandia. Although she had shared her house and her heart with Lord for only a few months, she knew that she had lost the best friend she had ever had.

Paquita returned home to a house that had never seemed emptier or lonelier. Even her invigorating beach walks no longer held the promise of rejuvenation without the presence of her faithful canine companion.

And then one day in June 1993, Paquita was startled to hear a familiar scratching at the French windows. Her heart beating rapidly, her mind wondering if her senses were playing tricks on her, she rushed to open the door.

And there was Lord, bedraggled, scruffy, with bleeding paws, asking to be let in just as he had done nearly eight months before.

Paquita broke down in tears. She remembered just hugging and hugging Lord, and he was so happy to be home that he couldn't stop licking her face.

Somehow, Lord had found his way home to southeastern Spain from Montpellier, France, a distance of more than 500 miles. He had worked his way across mountains, through forests, around dangerous highways to be reunited with his mistress. For five months, he had trekked down Spain's Mediterranean coast to return to the love of the gentle woman who had found him scavenging for food on the beach when he was a pup.

Muggins Made It Home after Eleven Years!

Late in 1991, Cheryl O'Connell of Lawrence, Massachusetts, was out gathering information for a new city directory when she thought she heard a familiar bark.

Reasoning that it couldn't be Muggins, the St. Bernard-collie mix that they had lost in the summer of 1980, Mrs. O'Connell had to investigate. To her complete astonishment, she beheld their beloved pet. Truly, it was as if Muggins had returned from the dead.

Muggins jumped up and began licking her mistress. After so long an absence, Cheryl O'Connell simply found this very hard to believe.

When Muggins had disappeared, the O'Connells had searched for months—everywhere they could think of—desperately seeking their pet. When they at last called off their hunt, they continued to pray that their dear Muggins was being well cared for.

Cheryl O'Connell soon learned that their prayers had been answered in the form of Henry and Rosemary Carrier, who had "adopted" the wandering Muggins—whom they called Brandy—ten years before. The Carriers had grown to love Brandy/Muggins deeply in that decade, so Mrs. O'Connell quickly saw the dilemma before her. After so much time, she simply could not ask the Carriers to surrender a dog that they had long since considered theirs.

However, this strange account of a dog that finally came home has a double-tailed happy ending. Since the O'Connells have three children—aged twelve to five—the Carriers decided that the fifteen-year-old dog would be better off in a home with kids.

The O'Connells are more than pleased to share Brandy/Muggins and her affectionate nature with the Carriers, though. And Rosemary Carrier often stops by with a special steak for the big St. Bernard-collie.

Lost Dog Recognized His Mistress on Television

Ciak, a German shepherd-collie mix, found himself in a most peculiar situation. His owner's cleaning lady had taken him for a walk—and for whatever reason had seemed appropriate at the time, he decided to run away. And then he found out that he was not one of those dogs who had the ability to find their way home across mountains, icy rivers and mammoth canyons. He couldn't find his way back to his mistress, Italian anchorwoman Alessandra Canale, through the streets of Rome.

Ciak finally made his way across the Eternal City and ended up at the front door of Monica Nannini, an actress, who took pity on the stray pooch and invited him into her home. The confused Ciak unhesitatingly accepted her hospitality, and he made himself comfortable in his place of refuge for over thirty days.

From the very beginning of his sojourn, Monica noticed that Ciak seemed to behave very strangely whenever a certain attractive blonde newscaster appeared on the television screen. He would immediately begin to bark and wag his tail. The actress laughingly assumed that the stray mutt had a thing for Alessandra Canale.

Interestingly, Monica knew Alessandra casually, but she had no idea that the newsperson had lost a dog or that she even owned a dog.

About a month after Ciak had moved in with Monica, the actress happened to run into Alessandra at a bar near the television studio. Jokingly, Monica told her about the stray dog's behavior whenever she appeared on television. Either the dog had a crush on Alessandra or maybe he had been lost by a woman with long blonde hair like hers.

Alessandra became very excited. She explained that she had lost a dog of the same German shepherd-collie mix that Monica described. She had searched the neighborhood for her missing companion, and she had placed posters in local stores and taken out ads in the newspapers. All without success.

The television personality said that she had accepted the sad fate that Ciak had been put to sleep, since stray dogs are only kept for twenty-fours by pounds in Rome before they are disposed of.

Monica invited Alessandra to come home with her and to have a look at a canine admirer.

Later, Alessandra told journalist Silvio Piersanti that she had known as soon as Monica had described the dog that it had to be her buddy Ciak: "I couldn't wait to put my arms around Ciak. As soon as Monica opened the door, Ciak jumped on me, almost knocking me down, and licked my face. It was wonderful!"

His Trucker Buddies Reunited Driver with His Dog

Sabre, a nine-month-old French poodle, received a lot of help negotiating the 1,700 miles that separated her from her owner. A convoy of tender-hearted truck drivers saw to it that the little dog was able to hitch a series of rides from Greene County, Pennsylvania, to Brownwood, Texas, to be reunited with fifty-two-year-old Johnny White.

In January 1991, Johnny, his wife Donna, and Sabre had been

driving on a Pennsylvania highway headed for Buffalo, New York, when their rig hit a patch of ice and slid over a cliff. Donna was killed instantly, and Johnny was seriously injured. Sabre was tossed about the truck's cab and left behind when the ambulance hauled away her owners.

Johnny was first taken to a hospital in West Virginia, then, later, flown to a care facility in Brownwood, his hometown. Grief-stricken over the loss of his wife, it was some time before his thoughts could turn to the plight of their beloved Sabre.

As he lay in the hospital bed recovering from his near-fatal injuries, Johnny began to grow depressed. Sabre, too, must be dead, he thought. He had lost both his beloved wife and his dear little dog.

A sympathetic dispatcher with his trucking company's home office in Springdale, Arkansas, knew that Johnny was bereaved and left with doubts as to the actual fate of his tiny French poodle. The dispatcher got on the radio and put out an urgent appeal on the truckers' network to see what could be found out about what had really happened to Sabre.

It was soon learned that Sabre had been found by rescue workers at the scene of the accident, trembling and crying in a corner of the truck's bed. She was taken to a local animal shelter, then transferred to a private home.

When Johnny White's plight was made known to Sabre's foster owners, they quickly surrendered the poodle to a trucker heading south toward Tennessee. From there, she was handed over to a driver bound for Little Rock, Arkansas. In Little Rock, she changed rigs again, this time to a truck with the destination of Springdale. Once there, Sabre was taken to the home of one of Johnny's closest friends.

It was left for Johnny's brother to carry Sabre on the last leg of the journey from Springdale to Brownwood.

Johnny will always remember that when Sabre first set eyes on him, she ". . . ran all over the place, turning flips and racing in circles all around my legs, yipping and barking. She finally jumped into my arms."

After three terrible months apart, an awful time of uncertainty and sorrow, Johnny and Sabre were back together again. And it wasn't long before they were back on the road.

But before they left on their first trip without Donna, they stopped at the cemetery and visited her grave.

Cat Follows Trail of Little Girl's Tears to Find His Way Back Home

In March 1990, four-year-old Aurelie Assemat nearly died when she fell from a relative's fourth-floor apartment in Grugny, France. Although she lay in a coma for a month and her parents feared that they would lose her, Aurelie finally awoke. Sadly, though, she could no longer speak, she was nearly blind, and she was paralyzed down her left side.

Desperate to find some way to enliven their little girl's tragic condition, Georgette and Jean-Louis Assemat hit upon the idea of giving her a cat. They were delighted to see that the green-eyed tabby seemed to lift their daughter's spirits at once. Aurelie named her new friend Scrooge, and they became inseparable companions.

Georgette and Jean-Louis were greatly relieved to see that they had found an antidote to Aurelie's loneliness. She would hug the cat and cuddle it all day long. And far from displaying the stereotypical feline aloofness, it was apparent that Scrooge loved Aurelie as much as she loved him.

In August 1991, the Assemat family left their home in Grugny for a vacation in the country. Scrooge seemed to like the countryside as much as his human family members did, but when it was time to go home, it suddenly appeared as though the cat had decided he liked the new environment a bit too much. The Assemats were packed and ready to return home, but Scrooge was nowhere to be seen. He had wandered off at the last minute and had apparently got lost.

Jean-Louis and Georgette called and called for the missing cat, knowing the heartbreak their daughter would experience if he did not return.

Finally, the hour arrived when they had no choice other than to begin the return trip home without their feline friend—and their daughter's dearest companion. Although Aurelie had lost her voice due to her fall, she cried for her lost Scrooge throughout the entire 600-mile journey.

The effects on Aurelie of losing her cat proved to be devastating. She did not eat; she did not sleep; she lay sobbing in her bed, staring at Scrooge's empty basket. Her parents were afraid that their daughter had lost all interest in life.

As the months went by, Aurelie grew ever more listless and despondent. When they had first returned from the country, Georgette and Jean-Louis knew that their daughter had kept alive a hope that somehow Scrooge would return to her. Although they felt that such a dream of reunion was an impossibility, they said nothing to dash Aurelie's faith in prayer.

Then, on July 9, Aurelie and Georgette heard a feeble scratching at their front door. Aurelie began to move her wheelchair toward the door with an excitement that she had not experienced for nearly a year.

When Georgette opened the door, they were astonished to behold a woefully bedraggled cat.

Then, for the first time since her accident, little Aurelie spoke: "Scrooge! It's my Scrooge! He's come home!"

The cat walked to the girl's side and rubbed itself against her legs. Scrooge had found his way across the 600 miles that separated him from the Assemat's home in Grugny. It had taken him nearly eleven months to do so, but he had accomplished what had seemed to Georgette and Jean-Louis to be the impossible.

Georgette remembered that she was hugging and kissing Aurelie as her daughter was hugging and kissing Scrooge.

But the determined cat had paid a terrible physical price to complete his odyssey. It was immediately apparent to the Assemats that, fighter though he was, Scrooge was on his last legs. They resolved to take him directly to a veterinarian just as soon as they had given him something to eat.

The veterinarian was advised to spare no cost to repair the rugged Scrooge, for the Assemats had received a firm realization during his absence that he was the best cure they could provide for Aurelie. The fact that she had regained her ability to speak at the very sight of her feline friend was an additional proof that Scrooge was Aurelie's most effective prescription for a more complete recovery.

Scrooge's proud tail had to be amputated. The veterinarian expressed an educated guess that Scrooge had caught his tail in a trap and had yanked it free so that he might continue his journey home to Aurelie. Scrooge had gained his freedom with such a desperate act, but he had also wounded himself to the extent that his tail was riddled with gangrene. He also required an emergency hernia operation.

A few months later—after extended Scrooge therapy—Aurelie was speaking in an almost normal manner, and she had begun to walk with the aid of crutches. Without Scrooge, the Assemats dread to consider what might have become of their little girl.

Some days after he had returned to their household, Aurelie had told her mother: "My love guided Scrooge home. He knew that I was crying for him, and he just followed my tears home."

Paddy Paws and Miszan—Two Cats in the "Almost Gave Up Hope" Category

Jane MacDimarid of Winnipeg, Canada, had assumed that Paddy Paws had forfeited all nine of his lives years ago when he vanished from her home one night in 1989.

Then in February 1994, Cathy Mieyette, a local dog groomer, found a "bag of bones" cat shivering in a garage fifteen miles away from Jane's home. Cathy fed the tattered cat, read the ID number tattooed in its ear, and contacted the Humane Society.

Within a few days, the ecstatically happy Jane had Paddy Paws back home with her. After a five-year absence, Jane truly thought that he was a goner. "But I think this really gives hope to people," she said.

On a winter's night in 1993, Greta Vinberg-Nielsen of Stockholm, Sweden, heard a strangely familiar sound at her front door. A shiver ran up her spine, because the doorknob was moving in the peculiar manner that her beloved cat Miszan caused it to jiggle when she would jump up and touch the handle. The eerie thing was that Miszan had been missing for six years!

However, much to her complete astonishment and great joy, when Greta opened the door, she saw Miszan looking up at her.

Miszan had the cool to act as though she had been absent for only one night, not six years. She walked straight to the refrigerator and used the foot pedal to open the door the way she always did when she was hungry. Then, after she had satisfied her hunger, she ran upstairs and curled up at the foot of Greta's bed—just as she had done every night before her disappearance in 1987.

Certain that it could be no other cat than her Miszan, but wishing to completely satisfy the grumbles of the skeptical, Greta examined the cat's hind legs and verified Miszan's identity by the old telltale scars that she had borne.

Greta had to admit that not everyone in the household was delighted with the prodigal's amazing return. Her new cat Missan was jealous, and the two of them were constantly fighting for dominance.

Ratona the Homesick Bovine Came Home

It would appear that homesick dogs and cats are not the only pets that can develop the mysterious homing radar that enables them to find their way back to their owners over unfamiliar terrain.

In 1963, Jorge Díaz of Funes, Spain, shipped one of his prize cattle to be placed on exhibition at a livestock fair in Bordeaux, France.

After a few days, Ratona the cow apparently became sick of the spotlight and homesick for the familiar pastures of Spain. She managed to break loose and find her way home over 180 miles of alien countryside.

Two Strange Reunions

Science has no explanation for these remarkable stories in which a dog's loyalty and love somehow enable them to find their owners in faraway places where they have been before. One such classic tale has often been told of the indomitable Prince, a collie-Irish terrier mix, and his master Jimmy Brown.

Brown joined the British army during the onset of World War I and left his family, including Prince, with relatives in Hammersmith, London, before he shipped off with the other doughboys to France. Brown was with the earliest British contingents to be sent over the English Channel, and his unit was soon in the thickest of the fighting.

After a time, he was allowed weekend leave from the horrors of trench warfare and permitted to visit his wife in London. When it was time for Brown to return from his brief respite in England to the blood, the mud and the barbed wire, Prince would have none of it. At first he moped, refused all food, and barely drank any water. Then he decided to do something about it.

Colleen Brown was shocked when she stepped out one morning to look after Prince and made the terrible discovery that he was nowhere to be found.

She looked everywhere. She had no idea why Prince would run off, and she dreaded having to break the news to Jimmy. She knew that her husband would be terribly upset to find that his beloved dog had disappeared, and she didn't want to do anything to demoralize the poor lad, knowing that he was suffering enough in the cold and wet trenches.

She decided to wait ten days before she made the formal declaration that Prince had, indeed, disappeared; and in those days she would exert every effort at her disposal to attempt to track down the missing dog.

Finally, having proved to be a pest to all of her surrounding family and neighbors, who had all grown weary of spending large portions of their free time searching for the collie-terrier, Colleen came to an understanding that the honest thing to do was to write to Jimmy and tell him the sad news: Prince had been unable to bear the separation from his master and had run off a few days after Jimmy had returned to the front.

Colleen's astonishment knew no bounds when she received a letter from Jimmy in which he informed her that his rugged buddy Prince was there with him on the front and sharing a damp berth in the trench.

In a way that conventional knowledge has yet to comprehend, Prince had somehow managed to negotiate the unfamiliar streets of London, conquer seventy miles of unknown countryside, and get himself across the English Channel. Since the channel constitutes a body of water no less than twenty miles across between England and France, it is unlikely that Prince swam across. In some way, he must have hitched a ride on a sailing vessel of some sort that would be docking somewhere near the spot in France in which his master was temporarily residing. Once he had managed to get all four paws on French soil, Prince was next presented with the challenge of making his way sixty miles to the frontline trenches where Jimmy Brown was on military duty.

According to the records of this remarkable case, the feisty collie-Irish terrier arrived at the trenches at Armentières at a time when the British line was undergoing a merciless barrage of heavy shellfire from the German cannons. Ducking bursting shells, dodging erupting earth, and evading deadly tear gas, Prince was apparently still able to pick up his master's scent among an army of half a million Englishmen.

All of Jimmy's trenchmates agreed that never had a dog been so well named and titled as Prince.

In the pages of his book *Dogs: Man's Best Friend*, Captain Trapman relates the account of Peter, a bull terrier, who somehow acquired

the knowledge of how to change trains and how to read complicated time schedules—even in the formidable mass confusion of the
Cairo, Egypt, depot.

About 1901, as the story goes, a British government official named
Jobson was stationed in Upper Egypt. Jobson was well known for his
taking great delight in bringing his dog with him wherever he traveled, and it was customary for him to bring Peter along with him on
the fifteen-hour journey to Cairo. Jobson's human companions were
often amused by the bull terrier's serious demeanor and the manner
in which he would settle himself comfortably in a train seat and
never once even glance out a window.

A career reassignment transferred Jobson to Damanhûr, a city
about three hours' travel time from Cairo. On one occasion, a situation arose in which it was absolutely necessary for him to leave for
Cairo immediately, thus making it impossible for him to bring along
his constant canine companion.

It would be difficult to say who felt worse in this awkward situation
since Jobson seemed to consider his bull terrier as much a facet of
his overall appearance as his necktie and briefcase. Although Jobson did his very best to explain to Peter that it was not his choice that
he must stay behind, he left a very grumpy and out-of-sorts dog in
Damanhûr.

And Peter was by no means content to let the matter rest. In the
logic of his doggy mind, he reasoned that Jobson must have returned
to their former home in Upper Egypt and, for whatever purpose, had
left him behind. Somehow he made his way through the streets of
Damanhûr and managed to board a train to Cairo.

Once Peter had reached that familiar destination, he managed to
change platforms, switch trains, and set out on the fifteen-hour ride
to their old post in Upper Egypt.

Although it had often been observed that Peter had never bothered to look out the window during his many previous trips back
and forth to Cairo from Upper Egypt, he uncannily knew when to
leave the train and where to go to search out Jobson's old haunts at
his previously assigned station.

Perplexed when he could not find his master anywhere around
the old station on business, Peter's bull terrier powers of reason next

convinced him that Jobson must rather be visiting some friends in Cairo. Without wasting any more time, Peter headed once again for the train depot and the long ride back to Cairo.

Fifteen or so hours later, Peter was poking his head in the doors of a number of Jobson's friends and acquaintances in Cairo.

"What on earth are you doing here, Peter, old man?" he was asked again and again. "Wherever is Jobson? And what are you doing here without him?"

When he was unable to find his master at any of his usual ports of call, Peter displayed visible disappointment. Where on earth, indeed, was that naughty, wandering master of his?

Incredibly, the resourceful bull terrier once again made his way back to the Cairo train depot, waited patiently for three hours for the proper train to arrive, and then entrained once more for Damanhûr.

Here, at last, the persistent Peter was rewarded for his tireless efforts in locating his master. Jobson had returned home and had been worried sick about the mysterious disappearance of his loyal dog.

Although this remarkable story may sound like an inspired piece of clever fiction, we are assured that all the details were confirmed by a careful inquiry conducted by Jobson and his friends, many of whom had observed Peter at various locations during his determined search for his master throughout Upper Egypt and Cairo.

People and Their Pets May Be Reunited after Death

The late Ian Currie, author of the book *You Cannot Die,* once said, "There is a good deal of exciting evidence to show that life after death exists for animals as well as humans—and that we are reunited with those pets with whom we shared an emotional bond on earth."

Our own research has discovered a great deal of evidence which indicates that just as there is life after death for humans, so animals live on, too. They may become our constant, loving companions beyond the grave.

Currie, who was a lecturer in sociology at the University of Guelph in Ontario, recalled a séance in which the spirit medium was in contact with a Frenchman who had died some years earlier. "The spirit communicator said that as soon as he died, he had felt the body of an animal nestling against his own. When he opened his eyes, there was his pet horse, who had died some years before him."

Currie went on to tell of another séance during which a clairvoyant was in contact with the spirit of a woman who said that within minutes of her death, she had been happily romping with her beloved dog, who had been killed several years earlier. The spirit communicator said that the dog was in perfect shape.

We remember a séance we attended during which an alleged spirit communicator described her reunion with a pet after the death experience. According to the spirit entity, "Suddenly, when I opened my eyes, there on my lap, gently purring, was my pet cat, who had died some years before. I hugged him, and he nestled his head against my face. It was so comforting to have him there."

It may well be that even in death, our pets will be our closest companions.

Albert Payson Terhune's Phantom Dog

Certainly one of the most beloved authors of dog stories, Albert Payson Terhune was a great animal lover who kept dozens of his four-legged brothers and sisters in Sunnybank, his estate near Pompton Lakes, New Jersey. Although Terhune's favorite dogs were collies, he did have one rather attractive crossbreed named Rex, who was completely devoted to the writer.

Rex was a very large dog with a vicious-looking scar across his forehead—a combination of circumstances which made him appear much more ferocious than he really was. And though he felt it his duty to bark at every guest who walked across the threshold, Rex would contentedly curl up at Terhune's feet as he sat at the typewriter creating another canine adventure for his legions of devoted readers.

Due to a series of unfortunate events, Rex was killed in March 1916, and the saddened Terhune wrote the very moving story *Lad: A Dog* as a tribute to the memory of his dear pet.

Many months after Rex's death, Terhune was paid a visit by Henry A. Healy, a financier, who knew how much his host had loved his big dog—but who apparently had not been told of Rex's passing.

Just before leaving that evening, Healy sighed wistfully and said, "Bert, I wish there was someone or something on earth that adored me as much as Rex worships you. I watched him all evening. He lay there at your feet the whole time, looking up at you as a devotee might look up to his god."

Terhune was shocked by his guest's comments. "Good lord, man!" he exclaimed. "Rex has been dead now for more than a year and a half."

Healy turned pale, but stood by the testimony of his own senses: "I can swear that he was lying at your feet all evening—just as I've seen him do since he was a puppy."

Some weeks later, a long-time friend of Terhune's, Rev. Appleton Grannis, paid a visit to Sunnybank, and after a stroll around the estate and a pleasant afternoon meal, remarked that he thought Bert fancied collies.

"That's true," Terhune replied. "In fact, all of the dogs that I presently own are collies."

Rev. Grannis frowned his disagreement. "Then what dog was it that stood all afternoon on the porch looking in through the French window at you? He's a big dog with a nasty, peculiar scar on his forehead."

While the author knew at once that it was his old friend Rex returning for another visit from the spirit world, Terhune thought better than to attempt to explain the situation to a conventional man of the cloth.

Terhune said that even the other dogs were able to sense the presence of old Rex.

One of the collies, who had always been careful to keep his distance from the big and tough scar-faced crossbreed, continued to skirt very carefully around the rug where Rex had always sat waiting for his master to sit down to write.

Love for Her Cats Drew Her Back from the Other Side

Some years ago, Eleanor Kravig, a reader of *Fate* magazine, the popular journal of the paranormal, shared an experience that she had undergone while doing graduate work at Hunter College. At the time, she was living in a home sponsored by the Lutheran Church and primarily run for Swedish women during their stay in New York City. The office secretary was a rather dour, frowning woman who appeared to find her only joy in life in feeding the stray cats in the neighborhood.

Eleanor decided to be pleasant toward Anna Hanson, the gloomy secretary, and after having made the effort to be friendly, she discovered that Anna was not such a drab and dull person.

Some time later, Eleanor learned that Anna had become ill and had been taken to the Little Sisters of the Poor, a hospital on Seventy-second Street next to the Frick Library where she was doing her research work. She was genuinely concerned about the secretary's well-being, and she kept resolving to stop by the hospital and bring her some flowers.

And then one evening at dinner, Mrs. Karlson, the director of the Women's Residence, announced that Anna Hanson had died.

Eleanor was shocked and remorseful. "Only a few days before, she had sat there . . . perhaps controlling an intolerable pain under a gruff exterior. At least I could have gone to visit her and brought her a bunch of flowers . . . Now it was too late!"

A few days later when Eleanor came home from her studies, she clearly saw Anna Hanson feeding her cats.

"As she turned to smile at me, the face I saw was young and happy, a beam of joy transfixing every feature," Eleanor wrote. "Then she was gone. Only the hungry cats remained."

Eleanor Kravig concluded her sharing with her hope that somehow Anna Hanson knew of her concern and that her sincere regret had been felt on the other side.

Drowned Boy Brought Back to Life by the Spirits of His Dead Dog and Cat

William Serdahley, professor of health sciences at Montana State University Department of Health and Human Development, told writer Esmond Choueke of the remarkable near-death experience of a seven-year-old boy who was brought back to life by the spirit of his dead dog.

It seems that the boy, who was named Pete, went fishing off a bridge one afternoon. According to the friend who had accompanied him, Pete lost his footing while casting his line and had fallen into the river. As he plunged beneath the surface, he had struck his head on a rock and was knocked unconscious.

By the time his friend had returned with help, Pete had lain submerged at the bottom of the murky river for five to ten minutes.

A policeman managed to find the boy's body, bring it to the surface, and pull it to a river bank.

But by this time, Pete had no pulse and his respiration had ceased. By all appearances, the boy was dead.

What his rescuers could not know, however, was that the seven-year-old Pete was in the midst of an out-of-body, near-death experience.

Later, after he had been revived, Pete told Professor Serdahley that he had been floating in a special kind of place, a place where he had never been before. He floated into a tunnel, and he became somewhat frightened when he drifted deeper inside.

"Then I saw my old dog Andy and my old cat Abby come over to me in the tunnel," Pete said. "I was really happy to see them, because I hadn't seen them since they died a long time ago."

Andy and Abby were just as nice as he had remembered them, and Pete began to feel a lot better just knowing that they were with him. He no longer felt alone or frightened.

Andy, his beloved dog, drew closer to Pete and licked his hand.

"I petted him," Pete said. "Then he put his head right by mine and began to lick my face."

And that was what had made Pete come back to his "regular body" and to wake up "in a hospital with people all around me."

Pete was examined carefully by a number of doctors and, thankfully, was found to have suffered no permanent damage, mental or physical, from his near-death experience at the bottom of the river.

Professor Serdahley expressed his opinion that "when Andy the spirit dog licked his face, it was a signal that Pete should return to his body. Andy was telling him it wasn't his time to die yet."

Goldie Came Back from the Dead to Save Her Family from Fire—for a Second Time!

Mark and Donna Draper, who live in a suburb of Atlanta, believe that their hero dog Spanky is the present incarnation of Goldie, who saved them from a blazing inferno in 1991.

During their first ordeal by fire, the Drapers were awakened during the night by the barking of Goldie, their golden retriever.

"It was about four in the morning when Mark and I awoke to find Goldie standing at the foot of our bed, barking and jumping up and down and tugging at the sheets," Donna recalled. "Then he ran up to our three kids' rooms and woke them up."

By this time, the house was so thick with smoke that the Drapers could hardly see a thing. But Goldie kept at them, barking frantically until each family member had been guided to safety.

But Goldie had sacrificed himself for the lives of his family. The Drapers were devastated when he died a few hours later of smoke inhalation.

After they had rebuilt their home, the Drapers went to the dog pound in search of another golden retriever to take the place of the noble Goldie. They found a homeless dog that filled the bill, adopted him, and named him Spanky.

From the very first, there were astonishing similarities between Spanky and Goldie that seemed to stretch the bounds of coincidence just a bit too far.

There was, of course, the physical resemblance. Donna had at once noticed Spanky's "sweet face" that looked so much like Goldie's that the entire family had warmed to him.

More remarkable was the fact that both Spanky and Goldie indulged an unusual taste for broccoli. And Spanky howled every time he heard country music—just like Goldie did.

Then, in 1993, the Drapers suffered another house fire—and Spanky conducted himself in the same courageous manner as Goldie had done.

"It was uncanny," Mark Draper commented. "Spanky ran around the house barking and carrying on, just like Goldie had done."

This time, however, *all* the family members were saved from the fire—including Spanky.

Spanky's unselfish behavior during the fire was the deciding factor in convincing the Drapers that he was the reincarnation of their beloved Goldie: "They both put our lives ahead of their own in the face of danger!"

Her Cat Keeps Reincarnating and Coming Back to Her

Sonja Haralds of Reykjavik, Iceland, told us that she loves her pet cat all the more because he keeps reincarnating and coming back to her, "more sweet, more lovely, and more beautiful each time."

Sonja said that the ring of return with her beloved cat began when she was just a girl of five. At that time, he was a black male cat, and she didn't meet him in another incarnation until she was twenty-four years old. This time he was a black and white female, and Sonja named her Whiskey.

Sadly, some cruel and thoughtless person poisoned Whiskey, but she came back a few years later as another black and white female whom she christened Tipsy.

"Tipsy went looking for me when I went abroad on a holiday," Sonja said, "and she disappeared."

Then, while visiting America in 1974, she got her cat back in the embodiment of Puff-Puff, a male.

"Although Puff-Puff was brave enough to chase a big German shepherd off our lawn, he was otherwise a sweet and gentle cat," Sonja told us.

Puff-Puff also met a tragic end when he was put to death by the Humane Society in Boca Raton, because Sonja could not come back from Iceland soon enough to get him out of the pound and take him home with her.

Back in Iceland, though, the loving cat's spirit returned to Sonja as Keyhole, "sweet and gentle, helping to take care of ten kittens with the two other cats we also owned." The tender Keyhole was struck and killed by a car, and Sonja said that she "cried for a long time."

But then—"Sarai was born to us on May 22, 1991, the only long-haired and all-black kitten among six in the litter."

Three months later, Sonja had to leave for Portugal, but when she returned after an absence of eight months, Sarai still recognized her.

"On May 10, 1993, she had her first three kittens, all short-haired, and I hope and pray that she will stay with me for a long, long time. I have been told that she is the embodiment of the cat on the Tarot card of the Queen of Wands.

"I hope that my story will help animal lovers all over the world who mourn a beloved pet," Sonja concluded. "Because they may come back to you."

Pets Make Great Ghostbusters

Our famed colleagues, Ed and Lorraine Warren, have gained an international reputation as psychic investigators and exorcists. One of their more publicized investigations occurred in the apparently demonically possessed house in Amityville, New York, that has become notorious as the "Amityville Horror." The eerie manifestations in that house have spawned a series of motion pictures dramatizing the bizarre occurrences that drove the homeowners out of the blighted domicile.

Drawing upon more than forty years' experience as ghostbusters and demonologists, Ed and Lorraine have noted that animals appear to have more highly developed psychic powers than humans.

"If a home has a ghost's presence, our dogs will spot it first," they told writer Earl Stresak.

After they had investigated the spirit-afflicted house in Amityville, Lorraine remembered that a ghost had followed them home.

"I had gone to bed when my small terrier began to growl and stare at one spot near the bed," Lorraine said. "Its hair stood on end, and it bared its teeth. I knew that the terrier was looking at a presence that I couldn't see.

"A moment later, I could feel the spirit's presence. But the dog had become aware of the ghost first and had actually seen it."

The Warrens used to own a Belgian sheepdog and a Border collie that they would always take with them whenever they were asked to call upon a haunted house.

"If there really were ghosts in the house," Lorraine said, "the dogs would always begin to growl and their hair would stand on end. I believe that most average dogs will react in a similar manner when confronted with ghosts."

Ed agreed, adding, "Most of nature's animals have very keen psychic powers. That definitely includes cats—and even snakes."

Simba Sensed the Power of Evil from Thousands of Miles Away

In our book *Strange Powers of Pets*, we relate a number of personal experiences in which our pets were sensitive to the vibrations of ghosts in so-called haunted houses. In one instance, however, our dog seemed to pick up on vibrations of evil from thousands of miles away.

We had been conducting a telephone interview with the rugged actor Clint Walker, star of the television series *Cheyenne* and such motion pictures as *The Dirty Dozen*, who had been telling us about a mysterious attack that he had weathered from four eerie dogs that had seemingly manifested from nowhere. The dogs were strange-looking creatures, like no dogs that he had ever seen before.

Although he had managed to drive the dogs away, that night he had experienced an awful nightmare which required him to set his willpower against the dream's power and to call upon the name of Jesus to reject its negative energy.

"There are evil forces, you know," Clint told us. "I have learned this is so, and we must stay strong against them and not give them power over us."

As the actor had been completing his eerie tale, our old Lhasa apso, a fellow 'way up in doggy years, began to growl and bark at something in our darkened hallway. Truly, Simba never barked at anything—with the exception of a sharp yip when it was time to obey a call of nature. And now, he was growling and walking very cautiously toward something that he could sense or see in the dark corner of the hallway.

When our interview was concluded, we went out to investigate, but could see nothing. Simba, however, continued his nervous growling and his fixation on one particular spot in the hallway. He continued his vigil for nearly an hour before whatever it was that he sensed or perceived on some level of his consciousness had dissipated.

Had Simba somehow picked up on our conversation and in some manner received an image of those devil dogs that had attacked Clint Walker? Or had our conversation about the eerie and demonic brought some negative influence, some evil energy, temporarily into our own home?

Whatever it was, we had the courageous Simba to keep it at bay.

The Terrier Sniffed Out the Phantoms of Edge Hill

Barbara Kipling, who lived in Leamington Spa, Warwickshire, told author Dennis Bardens of the interesting reaction of their dog to a haunted site.

According to Mrs. Kipling, in June 1976, she and her husband joined with members of a literary society to visit an old church. Since it was a pleasant day, the Kiplings decided to let their old Jack Russell terrier out of the car to go for a run on top of the ridge after the formal meeting had disbanded.

The dog was totally enjoying her romp, sniffing about for rabbit scent, when she suddenly stopped frozen in her tracks. The Kiplings watched with great concern as their terrier, hair bristling, seemed to be running away for her life, tail between her legs. For a time, they suspected that she had been stung by some angry hornet whose turf she had invaded.

Three days later, the Kiplings had occasion to return to the site as a likely spot for their grandson to fly his kite. Absorbed in the lad's efforts to get his kite soaring, they were being inattentive to their dog —until they noticed that she was exhibiting the same peculiar behavior as she had before when they had visited the area.

Barbara remembered that the terrier once again seemed extremely distressed, and she finally became so obviously frightened that she ran off. When they caught up to her, she trembled and gasped until they were some distance from the hill.

The spot where the dog reacted in such a stressful manner happened to be an old Saxon burial place dating back to the sixth century, where, some years back, forty skeletons had been discovered. The Kiplings theorized that their old terrier was somehow tuning into the ancient energies of a haunted site.

At the same time, the dog may have been receiving rather more violent vibrations from the area, for that ridge is near the bloody ground where the famous Battle of Edge Hill was waged in 1642.

There seems little doubt that some locales definitely have built up their own "atmosphere" over the years and that such auras often give sensitive people (or their pets) feelings of uneasiness, discomfort— or even fear. Whether this may be caused by a psychic residue or by an impression of the actual event in the so-called psychic ether is a question that remains presently unsolved.

Psychically restored battle scenes offer excellent examples of what appear to be impressions caused by the collective emotions and memories of large groups of people under terrible stress; and perhaps the best known, most extensively documented, and substantially witnessed of such restored scenes was the phantom battle of Edge Hill, which was "refought" on several consecutive weekends during the Christmas season of 1642. The actual battle was waged near the village of Keinton on October 23 between the royalist army of King Charles and the parliamentary army under the Earl of Essex.

The desperate encounter had resulted in defeat for King Charles, and the monarch grew greatly disturbed when he heard that two ghostly armies were determined to remind the populace that the parliamentary forces had triumphed at Edge Hill. The king suspected that certain parliamentary sympathizers had fabricated the tale to cause him embarrassment, so he sent three of his most trusted officers to squelch the matter.

However, when the emissaries returned to court, they swore oaths that they themselves had witnessed the clash of the phantom armies. On two consecutive nights, they had watched the ghostly reconstruction and had even recognized several of their comrades who had fallen that day.

It is little wonder that the Kiplings' sensitive Jack Russell terrier felt so terrified and confused when confronted by such an amalgamation of powerful psychic energy at Edge Hill.

Marvel's ESP Saved Two-Year-Old Perched on Tenth-Floor Ledge

It seemed a day like any other in March 1993 when Caroline Ewing of San Diego was out walking Marvel, her golden retriever in a park near their home.

Suddenly the big dog seemed to freeze in mid-stride. His ears stood up, as if listening to a sound unheard by Caroline, and his hair bristled.

And then, according to Mrs. Ewing, Marvel started "going wild." Contrary to his usual habit pattern, he definitely wanted to cut short his walk in the park. He kept turning toward their apartment building, pulling and tugging, as if he wanted to return home immediately.

Startled by her dog's uncharacteristic behavior, Caroline found that she could do little other than be dragged along. She tried holding firm to the leash and redirect Marvel back on his walk, but he totally disregarded her efforts.

She tried everything she could think of to calm Marvel down, but nothing could dissuade the big dog from his desire to return home. Caroline was completely baffled, because Marvel had been trained to obey her slightest command.

"But on this day, he paid no attention to me," she told reporter Richard Hopkins. "He was intent on dragging me back toward my apartment."

Once they were inside the apartment and Marvel was free of the leash, he ran into the nursery in which Caroline's two-year-old daughter Natalie was supposedly taking a nap. Then, while Caroline watched in total astonishment, Marvel went out through an open window.

She could only assume that her beloved dog had gone berserk and had leaped to his death, for the Ewings' apartment was on the tenth floor.

When she leaned out the window to confirm Marvel's whereabouts, Caroline received the worst kind of shock a mother could ever imagine. There, teetering precariously on a narrow ledge about twelve feet from the window, was her infant daughter Natalie! And there, slowly inching his way toward her, was Marvel.

This was truly one of those nightmarish moments when a mother's heart almost stops. Caroline felt helpless to do anything other than to watch Marvel ease his way cautiously along the ledge, painstakingly making his way to Natalie.

At last the brave, selfless retriever had the little girl by her diaper. Once the fabric was firmly clenched in his teeth, Marvel began the delicate task of slowly inching his way backward, dragging the baby one hesitant step at a time to the window and the safety of the nursery.

"My heart was in my mouth the whole time," Caroline said. "I knew that one misstep was all it would take, and Natalie and Marvel would fall to their deaths."

Once Marvel had brought Natalie safely back inside the apartment, Caroline had time to wonder about the whereabouts of the baby sitter whom she had left to watch the tot while she took the dog for his walk. A quick search of the apartment located the sitter, a neighbor who suffered from diabetes, collapsed and unconscious from a blackout caused by her disease.

Caroline immediately dialed 911, and a squad of paramedics soon arrived to attend to her neighbor's medical crisis.

Convinced that it was her dog's psychic powers that alerted him to the plight of both Natalie and the stricken baby sitter, Caroline declared that ". . . everything worked out wonderfully because Marvel insisted that I return home immediately. He's a real hero!"

The Flanagans Have a Telepathic Connection with Pleiades

Patrick and Gael Crystal Flanagan, who live near Flagstaff, Arizona, have a dear friend who is named after the Pleiadian star constellation.

"Pleiades is a very special being who just happens presently to reside in a little dog's body," Gael told us. "She only weighs about four pounds, and she gets carried around in her own little basket. She has such a charming personality that she spreads joy and laughter everywhere she goes."

Interestingly, Pleiades is a vegetarian whose favorite food is snow peas. She has Gael take each pea out of the pod so she can eat them individually.

"She's so small that each pea is a mouthful for her," Gael explained. "Of course, her peas must always be fresh and organic when possible."

When the Flanagans purchase the snow peas for Pleiades at the supermarket or health food store, the little dog always barks at the cashier to insure that her peas are the first item to be checked out of the shopping cart.

"The checkers all know this by now," Gael said, "and they are always careful to look for Pleiades' snow peas in the cart before checking any other items. If perchance they forget to give her snow peas priority, she will be sure to remind them by barking loud enough to be heard in the next two check-out counters. This gives everyone within earshot a good laugh."

Patrick and Gael are so close to their little friend that Pleiades sleeps with them and is often a fellow traveler in their dreams.

"On one occasion I dreamed that I was in another space dimension, a kind of way station between lives, and I was being guided by a spirit into a large room similar to a ballroom," Gael recalled. "As always, Pleiades was with me in her little basket. The spirit and I entered through the glass doors—without opening them. Inside this room were many, many souls dressed in the costumes of their various time periods. Some were clothed as Egyptians, others were Indians, Romans, Aztecs, Mayans, and other cultures from earth.

"I asked the spirit guide why there were so few animals present in this place, and the answer that I received was that only very special animals make it to this point. Pleiades looked up at me and smiled."

Gael told us that she often had dreams of Pleiades accompanying her and Patrick on their space travels in dreamland.

"We also have a very good telepathic connection in 'real time,' " she said, "and one day this connection saved our lives.

"We were driving home one day when all of a sudden Pleiades stood up in her basket and started to make some very strange sounds. Patrick and I were so surprised that he immediately slowed the car down to see what was the matter with her. Pleiades' peculiar behavior had occurred just before we were going into a blind curve on a narrow mountain road. On the other side of the curve was a 100-foot drop.

"When we drove slowly to the other side of the curve, we were shocked to see that a tourist was sitting still in his automobile with the vehicle broadside to both traffic lanes. He apparently had chosen this spot to perform a very slow and deliberate U-turn in the center of the highway.

"Fortunately, because of Pleiades' alert, we were able to stop in time," Gael said. "If she had not made her strange sounds, we would have been going too fast and we would not have been able to stop. Pleiades apparently had been able to sense the danger and was able to alert us in such a way that Patrick responded by slowing the car.

"If it had not been for Pleiades," she concluded, "we might be living in that other dimension that I saw in my dreams. Patrick and I both hugged and kissed our little friend and we bought her five pounds of fresh snow peas that night!"

Haggard's Dream of Old Bob's Death

H. Rider Haggard may have been best known for novels of fantastic adventure, such as *She* and *King Solomon's Mines,* but he was also recognized by those who knew him well as a great lover of animals.

One night, according to his own account of the incident, the author was experiencing a terrible nightmare, and was greatly relieved when his wife awakened him, thus retrieving his consciousness from the grip of the dreadful nocturnal drama.

As he was awakening, the shadowy residue of the nightmare completely disappeared from his brain—but he experienced the strange phenomenon of perceiving yet another dream in those few seconds before he returned to full wakefulness.

He dreamed that Bob, a favorite dog, a black retriever that he had always prized for its good nature and its intelligence, was lying terribly injured in some brush near water. In Haggard's night vision, the dog was attempting to speak to him in words. Then, failing at verbal communication, the retriever transmitted the knowledge that it was dying directly to the author's brain.

Once again Haggard's wife brought him to full waking consciousness by asking him why he was making such weird noises. The author replied without hesitation that he had just had another dream that old Bob was dying and was trying to tell him about his plight.

Soon after his unpleasant evening of nightmares, someone brought Haggard old Bob's collar. It had been found on a railway bridge.

Three days later, the retriever's body was sighted in the river beneath the bridge. The author was saddened to learn that his night vision had been accurate. Old Bob had evidently been struck by a train and thrown into the brush near the riverbank.

Crooktail, the Amazing Feline

Dr. Franklin R. Ruehl, holder of a Ph.D. in nuclear physics and host of the popular television program *Beyond the Other Dominion* on the Science Fiction channel, chose a cat named Crooktail as the most amazing feline that he had ever met.

"Meow! Meow! I heard those characteristic feline murmurs a few years ago when my mother and I were getting into our Buick Regal parked on the street in front of our apartment building in a suburb of Los Angeles," Dr. Ruehl began his account. "We both looked around, but saw no signs of a cat. Then a small paw suddenly emerged from beneath the vehicle, and we saw that it belonged to a scrawny, orange-striped tabby, only about six months old."

Then, before the two of them had a chance to introduce themselves to their feline visitor, the little fellow hopped onto his mother's lap and gave her two quick kisses.

"He then proceeded to shower me with like—or should I say 'lick' affection," Ruehl continued.

"I noticed that his tail was permanently bent, due either to a congenital abnormality or an everyday accident. I dubbed him Crooktail and reflected on how hard life must be for a cat with a deformed tail, how he might never find a warm sanctuary. However, before Crooktail left the confines of our auto, he had completely charmed us with his warm adorability.

"Crooktail didn't know that he was a deformed specimen of felinity, that his bent tail made him a laughingstock among other cats. All he knew was that he was a creature with an abundance of love to share. He and I became fast friends."

Ruehl subsequently learned that Crooktail had recently moved into the neighborhood with his human family and had quickly endeared himself to every youngster (and oldster) on the block.

One sunny morning a few weeks later, Crooktail jumped on Ruehl's shoulder as he was getting behind the wheel of his car, about to head for an important meeting relating to his television show.

"Normally, after a series of tickles on his head and a few strokes on his belly, Crooktail would be on his way," Ruehl said. "But on this occasion, he would not leave."

Ruehl was rather astonished when Crooktail began to cling to his coat and would not allow himself to be easily disengaged.

"Just then, virtually out of nowhere, an ancient pick-up truck with obviously faulty brakes passed by," Ruehl recalled. "The driver was apparently fighting for control of the broken-down relic, finally bringing it to a screeching halt at the end of the block.

"It was only then that Crooktail left me and darted off. Had he not delayed my departure, I would without question have been rear-ended by that truck, possibly sustaining serious injuries.

"While I may not be able to prove with absolute scientific certainty that Crooktail had a premonition of danger and acted to protect me, I would certainly not bet against it!"

We must make a strong point here that it is easy for us to assume the reader understands: Pets are as varied in their intelligence and their ability to invoke psychic abilities as are humans.

Although we hear from many men and women who contact us to share their own accounts of lost pets finding their way home or saving their human owners from floods or fires, there were also those who complained that their dog or cat or other pet seemed incapable of any task more complicated than eating and going for a walk. Well, sadly, we know that there is also quite a range of abilities among our human brothers and sisters. Humans do not all have the same IQ or have the same career aspiration or excel in the same sport.

When we were college and high school teachers, we always admonished our students when we assigned essays that they must narrow their topics, they must be selective in their presentation. As authors, we, too, must narrow our topic and present those stories about extraordinary pets with unusual abilities that defy current scientific elucidation.

We are quite aware that against all the stories of dogs and cats who have miraculously found their way home across hundreds of unfamiliar miles are the Lost and Found columns in any city newspaper that list rewards for dozens of pets who apparently were unable to find their way home from the park. But would you have wanted to read a book about animal klutzes who can't find their way home, about cowardly pets who fled their homes and left their human families to roast in flames, or about wimpy pets that can't survive hunger from breakfast to dinner? Of course you wouldn't. No more than you would want to read about the ice skater who was eliminated at the lowest level of the Olympic tryouts rather than the gold-medal winner, the high school dropout who can never keep a job rather than the self-made person who rose from poverty to head a major corporation, or the policeman who hid in his squad car when a robbery was in progress, rather than the officer who heroically and singlehandedly halted a bank heist.

Victim of Hunter's Bullet Sends Psychic "SOS" to Mama Dog

Kim Jackson of Ashville, Alabama, hadn't been too concerned when Teufel, their rottweiler, hadn't come home for dinner, but their terrier Truffles was becoming more agitated by the minute.

Kim started to become a bit worried. After all, it was the middle of deer-hunting season, and their house was located near hundreds of acres of very dense woods.

And she knew that Truffles and Teufel had a very special connection. Fifteen months before, Truffles and the Jacksons' rottweiler Zelda had delivered pups at the same time. Since Zelda had birthed fourteen "kids" and Truffles had produced six, they had decided to take one of Zelda's sons and allow the tiny terrier to be its surrogate mother.

Truffles had immediately taken to the pup and raised it as her own. Teufel made an instant transfer of his affection, and fifteen months later, the female terrier, less than half his size, was still his "mama."

It was becoming increasingly apparent that Truffles sensed that something was wrong with the missing Teufel.

"We had no idea that our lovable Teufel had been seriously wounded in the shoulder by a hunter's bullet—but Truffles sure knew something was wrong!" Kim Jackson said in the March 9, 1993, issue of the *Examiner*. "Somehow she suspected that Teufel was battling for his life. He struggled bravely, trying desperately to drag himself home with a grapefruit-size wound still gushing blood."

The Jacksons finally decided to let Truffles out of the house. The determined terrier hesitated for just a moment, as if tuning in her canine "radar," then she ran straight for an unused dog run where Teufel had played as a puppy.

After a few moments, Kim heard a piercing howl coming from that direction, and when she caught up to Truffles, she found her sitting next to the ". . . limp, blood-covered body of Teufel."

At first Kim feared the young rottweiler was dead, but upon closer examination, she saw that his chest was still moving slightly.

She called for other family members to come to help her, and the Jacksons rushed Teufel to a veterinarian twenty miles away.

While the veterinarian worked for hours to stitch up the rottweiler's wound and stop the bleeding, back near the Jacksons' home, Truffles maintained a vigil next to the bloody patch of grass where they had found the injured Teufel. She had been joined by Zelda, Teufel's biological mother, and the two of them began a mournful chorus of distress over their wounded son.

Late that night, Kim Jackson said, Teufel began a dramatic recovery. "Incredibly, at the instant his condition turned around, the two mother dogs stopped their mournful howls and came home."

As if they had somehow been transmitting psychic healing to the injured Teufel, the two moms seemed to perceive that the crisis had been passed. They ate and drank for the first time in over six hours, and they even lay down beside each other and permitted themselves a brief nap.

It is Kim Jackson's belief that somehow, mysteriously, "the same psychic power that drove Truffles to find Teufel in the woods" was the same mystical energy that informed both dogs that their son was going to be all right.

"In fact," she concluded her account, "he's doing great now and will recover completely, thanks to the vet and to Truffles!"

Just How Did Their Psychic Cat Manage to Ring the Doorbell?

Reverend Bob Short, who lives with his family in the high desert country of Southern California, had always told his wife and children that the only time that they could keep a cat in their house was if they found one wandering homeless and helpless in that rough country.

"I had primarily directed such stringent requirements to our daughter," Bob told us, "because she would have turned our house into a menagerie if I had allowed it."

But it hadn't been very long after he had uttered the decree when members of the Short family happened upon a small baby kitten one night while they were out walking.

"It appeared to have been dropped accidentally by her mother on the way to its home," Bob said. "I took one look at this small creature and knew that we were going to be old and close friends. And as the kitten grew in size, it also grew very close to the family and more particularly to me. He would wait for me to arrive home, then he would jump up onto my shoulder and purr contentedly, as though he were saying, 'I am happy to see you home.' "

It wasn't long before the Short family began to notice that the cat could apparently read their minds.

"We would only have to look at him and ask if he were hungry or wanted to go outside, and he would either go to his dish or to the door. We also noted that when we wished him to come home for the night or for his evening meal, we had only to 'think' strongly on these matters, and within five to ten minutes he would come over the fence and arrive at our door—then cry out to be let in."

Kitty-Kat, as he came to be named, would sometimes ask to be let out shortly before the human members of the family wanted to go to bed.

"When it happened that he was still out and we fell asleep, one or another of our family would be awakened during the night by a dream of Kitty-Kat wanting to be let in at the door," Bob said. "It never failed when the dream so motivated one of us to get out of bed and investigate, Kitty-Kat would be standing there, waiting to be let in. It appeared that he could telepathically 'invade' our dreams with his desires."

One morning when Bob was soundly sleeping, he was greatly annoyed to be awakened by the sound of their front doorbell ringing loudly.

"I sleepily glanced at my alarm clock, saw that it was three o'clock in the morning, and staggered to the kitchen wondering who would *dare* to ring our doorbell at such an ungodly hour of the night.

"I flipped on the solarium light which illuminates the front door, then very warily stepped to the door and peered out. At first I saw no one, then I spotted Kitty-Kat standing there just before he started to cry out, as though to say, 'Well, here I am. Aren't you going to let me in?' "

Bob looked down at Kitty-Kat and said to no one in particular, "But the doorbell? What in the world?"

Then he watched his cat as he casually moved through the door and into the solarium. "Kitty-Kat," he asked incredulously, "just *how* did you manage to ring that doorbell?"

To this day, Rev. Bob Short told us that he doesn't know if Kitty-Kat somehow managed to jump up and hit the doorbell button several times in a row—or if the psychic cat managed to use mind over matter to ring the bell.

Chris Proved His ESP in the Laboratory

Chris, a mongrel dog, was always eager to display his ESP abilities in the home of his owner, George Wood. Chris could tap to fourteen on command and would add totals when asked to do so. For instance, if a visitor to the Wood home should ask Chris to add three and three, the dog would unhesitatingly tap out six beats with his paw.

Dr. J.B. Rhine, the "father of parapsychology," tested Chris for ESP abilities in his laboratory at Duke University, and because some skeptics had suggested that Wood was somehow signaling the answers to Chris, the dog's owner was excluded from the room. It didn't take long to determine that Chris was responding to his interrogators' questions on his own. And soon he was replying to queries that Wood—or probably any other human—would be unable to answer.

On one occasion, Chris responded with accuracy to questions put to him by seven different interrogators. His talents for clairvoyance and precognition were explored when he was able to report on the scores of ballgames being played in different states.

Dr. Rhine decided to test Chris with the famous Zener ESP cards, which consist of five symbols—a square, a circle, a triangle, a cross, and wavy lines. A normal score would find the testee guessing correctly five out of the twenty-five cards in the deck. Chris very often scored fifteen out of the twenty-five.

Saved from an Avalanche by a Rescue Dog's ESP

During January 1951, most of Europe was paralyzed by heavy snowfall and blinding blizzards. The isolated Binn Valley, located twenty-five miles east of the magnificent Matterhorn mountain in the Swiss Alps, was smothered by a record snowfall.

In the mountains, such unexpected blankets of heavy snow almost always bring tragedy in their wake; for although the hearty and resourceful Swiss mountaineers usually make it a matter of regular procedure to plan carefully for the winter months, there will always be some families who remain ill prepared for such sudden storms—and there will always be unwary travelers and tourists who find themselves stranded and freezing.

Not long after the storm had struck with its full fury, a party of five men were delegated by their isolated families to go in search of firewood to prevent them all from freezing to death in their homes. It may have been a misstep, an inappropriate shout, or malicious accident that brought a roaring avalanche down upon the men and completely buried them under tons of snow.

A seventeen-man rescue party with a trained avalanche dog found the unfortunate wood hunters and freed four of the men, half-frozen to death, but still alive.

"Fritz acts as though there are more down there buried under the snow," one of the rescuers said, noting the dog's nervous sniffing and pacing.

The four recovered victims were wrapped in blankets and receiving first aid. Although the wood hunters were barely conscious, the leader of the rescue party approached the more alert member of the group and asked if there were others still covered by the snow.

The man blinked his eyes, sipped at the hot coffee, and looked carefully around him at his companions. "One more," he said. "We have one more of us."

The avalanche dog had not waited for human verification of the truth that his sensitive nose had already informed him, and he was already pawing through the fatal mixture of brush, rock and snow, sniffing out the location of the fifth wood hunter.

"Good boy, Fritz!" the rescuers shouted when the powerful dog uncovered the missing man. "Good job!"

A few minutes later, when all of the victims were receiving emergency medical treatment and thanking Fritz, the rescue party, and God that they had all been found while they were still alive, Fritz once again began to sniff the cold air and pace nervously.

"Good lord, is there yet another down there?" one of the rescue squad asked the dazed party of wood hunters.

"No, no," one of the men answered. "There were only five of us. We are all accounted for."

Fritz began to whine, and he bared his teeth to catch the fabric of the team leader's padded snowsuit. Once he had snagged a clump of the material, he began to tug at his master's leg.

"Fritz senses something," the leader said. "He wants us to get out of here—fast!"

Another of the team spoke up: "I've never seen the dog behave like that. If he wants us out of here, I think we should leave at once!"

The team leader gave the order to evacuate the area immediately and to move farther down the valley. "Pick up the injured men, put them on stretchers, and let's get out of here."

The seventeen-man crew and the five victims had barely moved to a safe spot when a terrible roar scattered the winter fog—and another snowslide, much larger than the one that had buried the wood hunters, thundered down the mountainside and completely filled the chasm.

Each of the men hoped that faithful Fritz, the avalanche dog with ESP, could understand how grateful they were of his warning of impending danger. They knew full well that not one of them would have come out of that massive, merciless avalanche alive if they had not heeded Fritz's desperate signals.

Canine Clairvoyants and Prophets

Jim, an English setter who belonged to a Sedalia, Missouri, hotel owner named Sam Arsdale, was one of those remarkable canine clairvoyants who also demonstrated an uncanny power of prophecy.

Beginning in 1929, the names of the horses running in the Kentucky Derby were written on slips of paper and fanned out before the setter seer. Jim would seem to spend a few moments considering the merits of the unseen horses, then he would place his paw upon his clairvoyant choice. Amazingly, according to Arsdale and numerous witnesses, Jim selected the winners of six Derbies in a row in this bizarre manner.

The astonishing Jim was tested by many prominent professors, who never seemed to tire of dreaming up new experiments in order to test—and possibly discredit—the unperturbed English setter. In each instance, Jim unerringly followed the pedants' instructions— even when they spoke them in several different foreign languages.

Summoned to the Missouri state legislature, Jim baffled the lawmakers by responding correctly to a series of instructions sent to him in Morse code.

Although the political pundits and pollsters picked Alf Landon as the winner in the 1936 presidential election, Jim picked Franklin Delano Roosevelt to occupy the Oval Office. When the remarkable English setter died in 1937, Roosevelt was president of the United States.

Although My Wee Missie could never claim the national attention achieved by old Missouri Jim, the purebred Boston terrier, who belonged to Mildred Probert of Denver, Colorado, did accurately predict Lyndon B. Johnson as the winner of the 1964 presidential election.

In the presence of reporters, Probert asked My Wee Missie, "If Johnson is the Number One man and Sen. Barry Goldwater is Number Two, who will win the election?"

Missie answered with a single bark.

When it was suggested that Mildred Probert reverse the question, Missie barked twice.

The little six-pound package of canine clairvoyance accurately told a *Rocky Mountain News* photographer how many children there were in his family and correctly distinguished their sexes. My Wee Missie also told *News* reporter Dick Roach the correct number of his brothers and sisters.

Communicating with Your Pets Through ESP

At the Tenth International Cat Show held recently in Madison Square Garden, there were more than 800 cats representing forty different breeds. But Lydia Hiby said that all she needed to pick up on a kitty's "vibrations" and understand what was going on in its mind was to be given its name and general whereabouts.

Lydia says that she is able to receive "picture messages" from cats, and she urges everybody to communicate with their own felines through ESP.

"You can understand cats," she told Marco R. della Cava of *USA TODAY*. "When they stare at you blankly, that's when they're reading your picture messages. It's better than TV."

Lydia, of Riverside, California, does not limit her telepathic conversations to cats. The thirty-five-year-old psychic sensitive says that she has made mental contact with dogs, horses, hamsters, birds, fish, lobsters, and even such creepy-crawlies as lizards and spiders. She estimates that such contact has enabled her to make the lives of 60,000 animals better by advising owners, trainers and keepers on how to improve the creatures' physical or mental health conditions.

She explained her modus operandi to writer Thomas P. Ramirez in the November 30, 1993, issue of the *National Enquirer:*

"The pet owner gives me the animal's name, and I talk to it mentally, trying to get images from it. I'll feel something in my body where the animal has a physical problem."

Lydia conducts up to thirty consultations a day, nearly half of them over the telephone from her home.

Mary Austin Kerns of Seattle, Washington, is another real-life Dr. Dolittle who appears to have the ability to communicate with animals on a psychic level. She compares the unusual talent to the same phenomenon as when a mother in another room knows that her baby needs her. In her opinion, the thoughts of animals have a pattern that is equivalent to a soundless voice.

Mary stays in practice by communicating with her four cats, three swans, twenty ducks, a dog, a horse and a turtle. Employed now as a pet therapist, she discovered her ability to "hear" the thoughts of animals when her cat surprised her by consoling her after the death of her parents in 1991.

Eliminate the Boundaries Between Animal and Human Life

The native people of North America seemed to have maintained a particularly close sense of union with the universe, its great dimensions, the invisible powers, the solar and lunar forces, the four cardinal points or directions. Today's practitioner of Native American medicine power retains a strong linkup between the human and the nonhuman occupants of the Earth Mother and works hard at establishing a great harmony with the various animals in his or her region.

The more that you permit yourself to become one with your pet, the more aware you will become of the world around you. You will begin to feel that you are a part of a much greater reality. And as your awareness grows, you will find yourself developing the ability to reach beyond your physical body and tune in on an intelligence that appears to fill all of space.

The more that you eliminate the old, rigid boundaries that have been erected between animal and human and allow yourself to experience the Oneness of all life, the more that you will find that communication with your pet can occur with a total disregard for distance.

. The cosmos operates according to sacred principles, whether you know, understand, accept them or not. When you start to become conscious of being One with an intelligence that occupies space, you will be able to tap that powerful energy and learn how to harness it with an increasing degree of success.

An Exercise to Achieve Attunement with the Cosmos and Telepathic Connection with Your Pet

Whenever you sit quietly in meditation, you are achieving at least some level of attunement with the Intelligence that fills all of space. Every time that you spend a few minutes in silent attunement with the cosmos, you are helping to undo the ancient restricting attitude that separates you from the Oneness of all life and from harmoniously blending your consciousness with that of your pet.

A good exercise to repeat on a daily basis to demonstrate your ability to join the seen and unseen worlds and to become more completely one with your pet is to stand with your arms stretched forward, your palms down, then intone the universal sound of Ommmmmmmmm in a long, drawn-out mantra.

Repeat this until you can actually feel tingling in the palms of your hands . . . until the skin actually begins to pick up auditory vibrations.

Then begin to project another type of energy to your palms. Try to project a life force to your palms. Visualize the life force passing through your fingers, moving out to the palms of your hands. Focus on this until you begin to feel a tingling sensation—almost as if electrical vibrations are moving through you.

Next, begin to feel an actual, palpable force moving out of your palms. When you have felt this force, begin to visualize a golden ball of energy hovering just beyond the palms of your hands. Visualize this as a great energy of love. At this time in your exercise, begin to project this force to your pet.

Visualize that golden ball moving toward your pet. If necessary, see it moving through the walls or through space to envelop your pet. Visualize the golden ball surrounding your pet with love.

To intensify the exercise, you may wish to visualize energy threads flowing out of your palms and touching your pet with connective energy. This is an excellent way in which to establish a telepathic connection with your pet.

Visualize golden threads moving out from the palms of your hands. See these golden threads moving through the room, through walls, through space if need be, connecting you with your pet. Visualize the golden threads moving and touching your pet. See the threads forming a network, creating an actual "telephone line" between you and your pet.

If you truly wish to develop an ESP linkup with your pet, first of all you must believe that it is possible to achieve such a harmony of psyches. Although we believe that such abilities are part of our natural heritage and may be achieved by anyone who sincerely wishes to develop these latent talents, there is no question that you must first believe that such phenomena truly exist. Once you admit to such a belief in mental communication, clairvoyance, telepathy and so on, then you must be persuaded to accept the possibilities of your own capabilities. In order to achieve deep levels of mental rapport with your pet, first comes acknowledgment, then comes awareness.

Another Exercise in Making Telepathic Transfer with Your Pet

Sit quietly for a few moments to still all of your senses.

Visualize the vastness of space. Contemplate the meaninglessness of time. Focus on the relativity of time.

See yourself as a circle that grows and grows until it occupies the entire area of your home . . . your yard . . . your block . . . your city. See the circle continuing to grow until it stretches across your state . . . your country . . . your world. Now see the circle reaching across the galaxy. See yourself blending with the Intelligence that fills all of space. See yourself melding into a oneness with All-That-Is.

Now clearly visualize your pet. See the pet plainly. Feel its presence.

In your mind, speak to your pet as if it were sitting there before you. Do not speak aloud. Speak to your pet mentally.

Breathe in comfortably deep breaths; this will give added power to the broadcasting station that exists in your psyche.

Mentally relay—then repeat twice—the message that you wish your pet to receive from you.

On the simplest level, this could be such a command as "Bring me the ball" or "Fetch the stick."

Give the pet a minute or so to respond. If there appears to be no immediate reaction, repeat the mental message two more times—or until your pet responds.

On a deeper level, this technique may be used to correct or to intensify any of your pet's habits—good or bad. In this case the command might be "Use your litter box!" or "Don't chew my shoes!"

You should never keep at this exercise until you are weary of it or bored. You must always maintain a fresh, enthusiastic attitude for best results.

After continued practice, the results you achieve will be quite dramatic, and you will have progressed much farther along the rewarding path toward establishing a firm telepathic linkup with your pet.

Part Two

INCREDIBLE FEATS OF SURVIVAL, ENDURANCE AND SUPER SENSES

There is no question that our pets can have amazing powers of endurance. A week after the legendary Johnstown, Pennsylvania, flood in 1889, a cow, a dog and five hens were found buried in mud under two freight cars—and still very much alive.

In March 1994, truck driver William Clark noticed a mature beagle staggering along a remote road near Mt. Olive, New Jersey. The dog's head was covered with blood, and the humane trucker pulled off the road to investigate.

It quickly became apparent to Clark that the beagle had been shot numerous times in the head. Some heartless creep had been determined to get rid of his old dog and had decided to shoot her and save himself the fifty bucks a vet might charge to put her to sleep. But four bullets hadn't finished the cruel job, and he had left her to die a slow death at the side of the road.

Closer investigation revealed that three slugs had struck the top of the beagle's head and remained lodged in the area between the skin and the skull. A fourth bullet remained behind her left eye.

Veterinarians said that the dog was at least twelve years old and, in the sight of her former inhumane owner, of no further use to him.

But four slugs could not put the tough old gal away, and the Humane Society soon received numerous offers of adoptions from admirers of the beagle that bounced back from death's door.

As an example to all future heartless dog owners who choose such a brutal way of ending their relationship with a pet, the police authorities and local animal lovers offered a $5,000 reward to learn the identity of the cruel gunman.

Author-educator Bergan Evans once remarked [*The Natural History of Nonsense*] that it was almost impossible to pass an evening in a group of ordinary, middle-class, well-to-do people without hearing of some instance of a dog's supernatural powers; and the least expression of doubt or the slightest attempt at cross-examination is sure to provoke a great deal of warmth. "Dogs are sacred in our culture and nothing about them is more sacred than their ability to foretell the future, to warn of impending calamities, and to sense 'instinctively' the death of a master or mistress who may chance at that moment to be far away."

You Can't Keep a Good Dog Down!

In 1990 when Iowa farmer Bill Davis ran over Rusty, his Australian red heeler, with a mower, he was horrified to see that he had pretty well mangled the dog's left legs.

The veterinarian had no choice other than to amputate Rusty's back leg below the knee and to leave little more than a stub of the front leg.

But three days later, the tough pooch was walking on his two good right legs. In another six weeks, he was able to jump into Davis's pickup just like he could before the accident.

Things settled back to normal on the Iowa farm as Rusty herded the cattle with a kind of rabbitlike hopping run on his two right legs. Then, in 1993, someone struck the Australian red with a pickup truck, breaking his front shoulder and crushing his good back leg.

But Rusty was still game. He had by no means lost his will to live. The vet put four pins in the injured back leg, leaving the dog with only one good leg to hobble on.

Bill Davis marveled at how Rusty maintained such a sweet disposition and displayed such great spirit. Never even for a brief time did he turn mean or bitter.

Early in 1994, when the vet removed the pins from Rusty's crushed back leg, the indomitable dog was immediately back to his determined self, earnestly herding cattle on Davis's farm.

Blinded and Burned, German Shepherd Survives Los Angeles Earthquake

Bimbo, a five-year-old German shepherd, was blinded and burned beyond recognition in an explosion that followed the devastating Los Angeles earthquake in January 1994. Although her owner, Jim

Menzi, had assumed that she had been consumed by the flames, she miraculously survived the deadly inferno.

Jim's truck had stalled at an intersection flooded by a broken water main during those frightening moments after the quake. His two canine buddies, Shep and Bimbo, were with him in the cab when he tried once again to start his vehicle.

What Jim could not know was that there was a natural gas leak nearby that had been caused by the tremors of the deadly quake, and when he turned the key in the ignition, the gas connected with the spark and exploded.

Instinctively, Jim jumped from his burning truck and into the water that surrounded it. He assumed that his dogs would follow his lead and abandon ship, but when he heard their terrible wails and yelps of pain and fear, he realized that the flames were holding them back.

Sadly, helpless to do anything to help them escape, all Jim Menzi could do was to pray that Shep and Bimbo would die as quickly and as painlessly as possible.

Later that day, when he was taken to a hospital, it was discovered that Jim had burns on 30 percent of his body. Rushed to intensive care, he mourned his dogs' fate.

"I kept replaying in my mind the nightmare explosion that had claimed my dogs," Menzi told journalist William Keck. "I could still hear their pathetic howls, and I cried for them."

But three days later, Jim received the astonishing news that Bimbo had somehow managed to survive the fire in the pickup. She had been found temporarily blind and completely helpless wandering in someone's yard, when a fireman noticed her and took her to a veterinarian. All evidence indicated that Shep had died in the fire.

From his hospital bed, Jim called the vet and inquired about his beloved Bimbo's well-being. The German shepherd had sustained burns covering nearly 70 percent of her body. She would have to continue to fight to live.

Jim gave thought to the humane consideration that it might be better to put her to sleep.

The confident veterinarian reminded him that the doctors at the hospital had not put *him* to sleep.

Inspired by the vet's bravado, Jim resolved that he would not allow

Bimbo to die. He arranged to talk to his dog via a speakerphone, and he told Bimbo that he loved her. The nurse who was with the German shepherd at the Blue Cross Pet Hospital said that every time Jim spoke, Bimbo licked her hand.

Both master and dog underwent similar treatments for their burns. As soon as he was released after sixteen days in the hospital, Jim headed for the pet hospital to be with Bimbo.

The attending veterinarians had shaved what patches of hair had not been burned in the pickup fire, and her paws were swollen and bleeding, but to Jim Menzi's eyes, Bimbo had never looked more beautiful.

Later, he told writer Keck that he had never felt a stronger bond with his dog. "Bimbo and I have been given the gift of life, and we're going to live each day for all it's worth."

Sadie the Flying Yorkshire Terrier

On September 13, 1993, a tornado touched down in Saginaw, Texas, and carried off shingles, siding, the usual assortment of debris—and one four-pound Yorkshire terrier.

Deputy Sheriff Sandra Davis of the Tarrant County Sheriff's Department received a call at work that the twister had struck her neighborhood, so she telephoned her husband James, an assistant manager at a local manufacturing plant; and the two of them rushed home.

They were commenting how fortunate they were that they had been at work and their eight-year-old daughter Lindsay had been at school when they noticed that Sadie, their dog, appeared to be missing.

Their shouts for Sadie soon reached their neighbor Mary Powers, who sadly informed them that she could solve the mystery of the missing terrier. According to her eye-witness testimony, the twister had picked Sadie up and carried her away. Ms. Powers said that she could see the poor little dog "being tumbled around like it was being bounced in a clothes dryer."

Although their house had sustained $60,000 in damage, the Davises' first concern was for their beloved Sadie. Frantically, they searched the countryside near their neighborhood, praying that, somehow, the tornado might have set the little terrier down safely somewhere in the area.

Freely expressing their sentiment that Sadie was a member of their family, the Davises sorrowfully had to call off their unsuccessful search by evening. No one wanted to put into words what appeared to be the realistic conclusion: They would never again see their dear little Sadie.

But a miracle was fulfilled the very next day. A man who lived more than two miles away called the Davis family to inform them that the dog that he had found after the storm was wearing tags that identified her as their pet.

Within minutes, Deputy Davis and her husband had driven the two miles that separated them from Sadie and they had reclaimed their windblown, but unharmed, Yorkshire terrier.

Duke Survived a Blast That Blew Him Out of the House

It was very fortunate for the DeCapitani family of Kenvil, New Jersey, that none of the human members of the household were home when the gas blast that leveled their home occurred.

Duke, their golden retriever, was home, though; and he was blown thirty feet into the air.

Witnesses in the neighborhood saw the Duke shoot through the front door like a cannonball. Part of his fur was enveloped in flame.

Police investigation soon revealed that a construction worker had accidentally ruptured a gas line. Before long the DeCapitani residence filled with fumes, which were eventually ignited by a pilot light in the house.

Duke was taken immediately to a veterinary clinic where he was treated for burns on his nose, irritation of his eyes, and a cut on his right front leg.

Although the vet pronounced that the hardy Duke would soon be fine, Walter and Jean De Capitani and their two daughters might not have fared so well if they had been home.

Kokomo Survived Twenty-four Days in the Subzero Winter of '94

The winter months of 1994 will be remembered as particularly brutal in the New England and Eastern seaboard states. Night after night the temperatures dipped into the bone-chilling subzero range. Those were not fit nights out for man or beast, but those were the frigid days and nights when Kokomo, a twelve-year-old shepherd mix, chose to undergo her twenty-four day ordeal.

The strange saga began on a night in early January when Carolyn and Terry Powers asked Terry's parents in East Meadow, Long Island, to "dog sit." When they returned to reclaim their faithful old shepherd, it became suddenly apparent that Kokomo had not really understood the plan. Sometime while the Powers were enjoying an evening out, the dog had jumped a three-foot chain-link fence and run away.

The Powers family conducted an extensive two-week search for Kokomo. They put up posters, placed notices in local newspapers, and contacted humane and animal care agencies in the area—all to no avail. They were all brokenhearted over the loss of their dog, especially the kids, Sean and Kelly.

But then, at 3:30 A.M., twenty-four days after she had disappeared, a very bedraggled and nearly frozen Kokomo was weakly barking at their door in West Islip, New York, asking to be let in to love and warmth.

The Powers family will never know why Kokomo ran away from Terry's parents to undergo a freezing hell on the run for more than three weeks. She returned to them as a "shivering skeleton" that had lost at least fifteen of her forty-five pounds.

Carolyn Powers recalled that as soon as they opened the front door to the half-frozen Kokomo, she "crawled straight under the bed."

Brandy Returned from the Grave—Literally!

In October 1992, Patricia Corcoran of Botwood, Newfoundland, realized that she had to face up to the sad fact that her ten-month-old mongrel dog Brandy had died of the illness that had afflicted her.

She had got her when she was just a six-week-old puppy, and Brandy had been a very good pet, loyally following Patricia and her daughters everywhere. But now, since she could no longer feel a heartbeat, she would have to accept the little dog's death as a sad reality of life.

Patricia asked a friend to assist her in Brandy's burial, and they chose a lovely spot near a waterfall. They dug a three-foot grave, said a few words, thought a few kind thoughts, and returned to Botwood.

Then, eleven days later, Patricia happened to catch a public service message on the local television station that described a lost dog that perfectly fit Brandy's description.

When she called the number and asked the man who had found the lost dog to call her "Brandy," he said that the dog had become very excited and began to jump up and down.

Patricia drove to the spot where they had buried Brandy, and she was stunned to find a hole in the grave, where the dog had apparently dug herself free.

When she went to reclaim her pet, Patricia was further stunned to learn that Brandy had been found only four days after she had mistakenly buried her.

The veterinarian who later examined the miracle mutt said that Brandy had only become unconscious prior to her premature burial. According to all body signs, Brandy was doing fine and bore not the slightest grudge that she had awakened in a three-foot hole covered with dirt.

Brownie Came Back from Doggy Heaven

It was one of the worst sounds that Mary Bratcher of Artesia, New Mexico, had ever heard in her life. The terrible, crunching noise she heard that March day in 1994 was the wheels of her truck accidentally crushing the life out of Brownie, their part-Chihuahua dog. Later, even worse than that sound, were the sobs and cries of her three-year-old son Toby, who refused to accept the reality of his doggy's death.

Even as Brownie was being lowered into his grave, Toby was sobbing his protest: "Brownie not dead! Brownie not dead!"

Someone's guardian angel must have been paying attention to the tragedy being played out in Artesia, for when the Bratchers returned to their ranch house the next afternoon, Brownie was waiting for them on the porch.

But the poor thing was a mess. He was covered with dirt, his right leg was broken, and one eye was hanging down his cheek.

Mary Bratcher found it hard enough to look upon their beloved pet in his wretched condition, so she wouldn't let her kids get close to him. She picked him up as gently as possible and headed for the veterinarian.

Although the vet couldn't save Brownie's eye, he saw no reason why the tough little guy shouldn't pull through. The doctor theorized that Brownie must have been in a coma and appeared to be dead when the Bratchers buried him.

Mary commented that she had had to bury a lot of pets in her lifetime, but this was the first time that she had ever had a resurrection. Jokingly, she said that she was considering renaming Brownie "Lazarus."

Dogs Who Work with Their Noses

Your pet dog probably can't see things as well as you can, and a dog's sense of hearing is not all that great—but when it comes to sniffing people, places or things, your dog's sense of smell cannot be beat.

As incredible as it may seem, a droopy-eyed, floppy-eared bloodhound has a nose that is up to three-million times more sensitive than a human's—and it can track a fleeing felon for more than a hundred miles and can locate missing people with a talent that seems almost supernatural.

How does a hound manage to track down and nearly always get his quarry? A human sheds some fifty million skin cells each day, and whether we can see them or not, we leave them scattered behind us in an invisible trail wherever we go. A dog, such as a bloodhound, can smell the microscopic organisms that feed on these skin flakes. If he has floppy ears, then so much the better to help him follow the scent, for his ears, swaying from side to side, fan the aroma of those tiny critters to his supersensitive snout.

The record for the ability to follow the oldest scent that had been left by a quarry is held by three bloodhounds—Doc Holliday, Queen Guinevere and Big Nose Kate. This terrific trio of trackers were able to pick up a scent that was nearly two weeks old, and they located a family of three that had been lost in an Oregon forest.

The record for the longest trail ever followed by a dog is 135 miles. A determined bloodhound picked up the scent of a burglar in Oneida, Kansas, and managed to pursue him to the far distant town of Elwood.

In what has to be a record of some sort, a hound named Boston rounded up twenty-three escaped convicts from the state penitentiary in McAlester, Oklahoma, in the astonishing time of thirty-six hours.

Choo Choo Is Able to Sniff Out Leaks in Roofs

Choo Choo, a three-year-old beagle mix, is contented to leave the long-distance runs and the rounding up of escaped convicts to the bloodhounds. According to roofing contractor George McKenzie of Stafford, Texas, Choo Choo can detect a leak in a roof nine out of ten times, which, McKenzie adds, is as good as any human can do.

McKenzie claims that Choo Choo can reduce the cost of repairs by as much as a thousand dollars or more, because, thanks to her remarkable talent, she can pinpoint the exact spot of the leak, thus preventing workmen from tearing up a larger portion of the roof in search of the problem.

However unexplainable it may be to conventional science, Choo Choo's modus operandi is simple and direct. Unassisted, she climbs up a ladder to the roof. She scampers about, sniffing here and there, until she smells rotting wood and mildew. Once she has isolated the trouble spot, she begins barking to signal McKenzie that she has located the leak.

Choo Choo's technique of drip-detecting when she is inside a house is equally interesting. According to McKenzie, she runs back and forth, looking up at the problem spot on the ceiling, as if she were measuring it.

Once she is satisfied with her inspection, she jumps up and bites McKenzie on the hip pocket, her unique method for indicating that she is now ready to go up on the roof. Once she is let outside, Choo Choo climbs up the ladder and heads straight for the rotted area on the roof.

Amazingly, McKenzie has observed, it is as if Choo Choo has some kind of tape measure in her head.

Howard Has a Nose for Arsonists

Howard is a two-year-old Labrador retriever who spent twelve weeks being trained by the Connecticut State Police K-9 unit to sniff out the cause of suspicious fires. Although modern technology has created some highly sophisticated equipment to evaluate each fire as a potential ploy by an arsonist, law enforcement officials have learned that a well-trained "arson dog" can detect possible criminal aspects of a fire even better than the gizmos of science.

Federal agent Charles Thompson gave the full credit to the dog's nose. He pointed out that laboratory equipment often misses such hard-to-detect materials as gas or lighter fluid that may have been used by an arsonist to create a destructive fire.

In the late summer of 1993, Howard and twenty-five other arson dogs were trained to investigate blazes throughout the eastern United States. Each dog is teamed with a veteran human arson investigator and each team is certified by federal agents.

Danny, the Exterminator, Tracks Down Termites

Dallas Pest & Termite Company claims that Danny the beagle is able to boast 100 percent accuracy when it comes to locating termites in their customers' homes. Brad Pitts, who works with the busy beagle bugbuster, revealed that they purchased Danny seven years ago from another firm for $20,000; but he vows that the eight-year-old termite terminator has been worth every penny of the price.

As any home owner who has ever been afflicted by the almost demonic manifestations of the terrible termite hordes knows, it is an almost impossible task to locate the little monsters once they have embarked upon their mission to destroy your home. Even highly skilled exterminators, who charge top-dollar for their efforts, can claim to be effective only about half the time.

But according to Pitts, Danny's superacute senses make him far more accurate than any two-legged bugbuster who is limited to poking around with a flashlight and a screwdriver. It seems that those pesky termites emit a scent all their own, and Danny is able to smell them and to pinpoint exactly where they have made their headquarters.

In addition to that super nose of his, Danny's sensitive ears are able to hear the clicking of the termite's ravenous jaws as they chomp through wood.

Once his nose and his ears have detected the little homewreckers at their awful work, Danny begins to paw the area in an excited manner, thus alerting Pitts and his coworkers to the bull's-eye on the termite target.

Super Snozzes That Sniff Out Drugs

In 1993 the townsfolk of Lansing, Illinois, got pretty upset when the local police department plunked down fourteen thousand of their tax dollars to purchase two German shepherds who had been trained to sniff out drugs.

Located about twenty-eight miles south of Chicago, Lansing is linked by a major interstate highway to the Windy City. Local officials had long suspected that their nice little city of 26,000 population sat right in the middle of a well-used route for the transportation of illegal drugs. The police had been steadily amassing conclusive evidence which indicated that couriers hauling huge caches of drugs and cash for various crime bosses were staying overnight in motels on the edge of Lansing, then hitting the highway and resuming their outlaw runs.

When police resentment over the brazen tactics of the drug dealers' couriers became known, certain citizens' groups protested that they wanted the police to forget about the creeps who were using their fair city as an oasis enroute to bigger scores in bigger cities. The concerned townsfolk wanted the police to focus attention on such local crimes as robbery and assault. However, Lansing police chief Dean Stanley had decided to put a stop to the drug traffic, and he acquired two German shepherds who had passed the course in illegal substance-sniffing with flying colors.

When word leaked out that the dogs with the sensitive snozzes would set the city back $7000 a head, Chief Stanley really found himself getting flack. And when it became known that police officers had to receive special training in order to handle the dogs properly and that the police cars had to be equipped in a special way to transport the German shepherds, irate citizens really started screaming.

One night in May 1993, however, one of the dogs, Prince, proved to one and all that he was much more than a pricey pooch.

A motel security guard called the police and requested the canine unit to check out a parked van with no license plates. Chief Stanley later told reporters that the keen-nosed Prince sat down and pointed his snout toward the area inside the van where he indicated that drugs were hidden.

"We quickly got a search warrant and found more than $5 million inside the van," Chief Stanley said. "It was wrapped in $10,000 bundles of $100, $50 and $20 bills."

Laboratory tests revealed that the bills tested positive for traces of drugs, but police officials admit that if Prince hadn't "told" them to be on the alert for drugs, they would have had no reason to search the interior of the van, and they would not have discovered the cache of cash.

Lansing mayor Bob West was pleased to announce to all naysayers, doubters and skeptics that Prince, the $7,000 dog, had turned out to be their $3 million canine benefactor. Under Illinois state law, the police were entitled to confiscate the van and to retain 65 percent of the illegal loot—a total of $3,382,057.25!

Chief Stanley explained to journalist James McCandlish that the remainder of the drug money, under state statute, was shared by the county and the state.

"We're going to bank the money and use the interest to build a new police firing range and to organize a drug-training program," he added. "And it's all thanks to Prince, the drug-sniffing dog."

Corky, USN, Says "No" to Drugs on Military Bases

In 1991, Corky the beagle was commended by First Lady Barbara Bush for his work in sniffing out illegal drugs on U.S. military bases. In only two years, the persistent dog nabbed 475 drug abusers to become the U.S. Navy's top dope-sniffing champion.

Interestingly, Corky had spent five years in the boondocks when it came to proving that he had any kind of useful talent in locating hidden caches of marijuana, cocaine, heroin and hashish. Cork proved to be downright cloddish and inept in finding anything other than his own dog dish at feeding time. During that time, the bungling beagle was almost drummed out of the corps, for his handlers had just about decided that Corky had absolutely no talent when it came to using his nose.

Then, in 1988, the mystical blend of pooch and people was discovered when Corky, the dunce of the drug-sniffing class, was turned over to trainer Joe Pastella and handler Burton Hunt. Apparently, love had been the crucial ingredient that had been missing from the dog's training schedule.

Almost at once, with Corky's attention to Pastella's training methods and his devotion to Hunt, the doltish beagle was transformed into the most amazingly accurate drugbuster in the U.S. Navy. Veteran trainer Pastella has hailed Corky's feats as nothing short of spectacular.

The twenty-eight-pound beagle has sniffed out as little as one seed of marijuana hidden deep in the seat of a locked car. He located a miniscule amount of cocaine secreted in a shaving kit that had been locked in a suitcase and buried beneath a pile of odds and ends in the trunk of a car. Corky has nosed out dope in people's pockets, cars, desks, apartments—even on their rooftops.

According to the authorities who work with him, Corky is never wrong and he never misses. His amazing talent makes a believer out of everyone.

Nicklaus Joins the Million-Dollar Drugbusters' Club

Ron Miller, canine instructor for the U.S. Customs Service, spotted Nicklaus, a large dog of mixed breeds, in an Athens, Georgia, animal shelter when the big guy was just one day away from being put to sleep and cremated. Seeking a dog that could be trained to retrieve objects quickly and boldly, Miller auditioned Nicklaus on the spot and decided immediately to adopt him and to spare him from the automatic disposal policy of the shelter.

Since his years of expertise as a dog trainer had enabled Miller to determine that Nicklaus possessed a very sensitive nose, he quickly established a program that taught the big dog to retrieve objects that had been scented with drugs.

As soon as the skilled canine instructor felt that his new student had been properly prepared for duty with the U.S. Customs Service, Nicklaus was assigned to work the streets of Hidalgo, Texas, with an experienced agent. Within a couple of months, he had sniffed out thousands of pounds of marijuana and millions of dollars' worth of cocaine.

The dog that was condemned to die in an animal shelter in Georgia soon made a big name for himself as an accomplished drugbuster in Texas. Nicklaus has been awarded with a spot in the Customs Service's Million Dollar Honor Club—and he was even presented with his own trading card.

The Incredible Wilderness Challenge of Irwin and Orient

Here is the wilderness challenge. Let's see how you would respond.

You are challenged to hike the entire length of the Appalachian Trail—that's a total of 2,144 tough miles through thick forests, waterfalls, rivers, mountain ranges.

And everything that you will need for daily necessities on the grueling trek must be stuffed into a ninety-pound pack on your back.

You say, no way? You say that the challenge sounds to you like something only an experienced camper and woodsman would undertake? And that then he would probably want at least two or three equally proficient outdoorsmen on his team, right?

When fifty-one-year-old Bill Irwin accepted the wilderness challenge, he had never hiked or camped before in his life, and his only companion was his *seeing-eye dog*, Orient.

Yes, that's correct. Bill Irwin is blind.

In March 1990, in perhaps one of the most astounding self-imposed challenges ever undertaken by a handicapped person, Irwin strapped a ninety-pound pack to his 210-pound frame and set out on the trail from Georgia to Maine. For the entire length of the arduous march, his only teammate would be his faithful German shepherd guide dog, thus proclaiming Irwin's confidence and trust in Orient's intelligence and resourcefulness.

The two adventurers began their trek in Dahlonega, Georgia, on a day when a driving rain sent a chill through them.

When they made camp on the first night, Irwin had no way of determining if they were lost or on the correct path.

With only Orient to guide him and no other human to read a map or to confirm directions, Irwin knew that he had no choice but to continue walking with firm determination.

That first night Orient curled up next to him, barking or growling whenever he heard the strange night sounds of wild animals in the forest. The big dog would continue to lie protectively next to his owner on every subsequent night of the wilderness journey.

On the third day of their trek, they chanced upon some hikers, who, much to Irwin's joy and peace of mind, assured him that they were, indeed, following the Appalachian Trail.

To some degree, Irwin had been able to prepare himself for the ordeal by listening to cassette tapes which described the wonders of the famous trail. Friends who had some familiarity with the area also did their best to paint substantial word pictures of the various terrains that they would encounter.

Irwin and Orient had not been on the trail too long before the German shepherd developed painful, running sores on his back from carrying a supplementary pack.

Irwin knew that Orient needed time to heal, so he added the dog's pack to his own.

For three weeks, he recalled, he lugged Orient's pack, struggling along, stumbling, being tripped by roots and knocked down by low tree branches.

Irwin admitted that he had felt genuine fear when a late-season hurricane came roaring inland from the Atlantic Ocean.

He remembered the wind howling, tearing branches from the trees, and ripping the trees themselves from the ground. While the lightning and thunder seemed to shake the very ground around them, the adventurer and his loyal canine companion huddled under Irwin's poncho.

Weeks turned into months as the stalwart duo maintained a steady pace along the trail. Occasionally, they would meet other hikers, who would confirm or deny the correctness of their course.

According to a prearranged plan established with friends, Irwin and Orient would leave the forest every five days to pick up food that had been shipped to designated post offices.

About halfway on the 2,144-mile hike, a misstep on a slippery rock in a river bed sent Irwin sprawling. The awful snapping sounds and the sharp pains in his torso provided him with the unwelcome news that he had broken several ribs.

For the next two weeks, Irwin said, each step, each breath brought him severe pain.

To make matters worse, he had already lost all of his nails from his toes rubbing against his boots while edging his way down long, steep stretches on the trail.

There were some days, Irwin concedes, when he assessed his broken ribs, his painful feet, the discomfort of cold, wet weather, and began to laugh at himself. But, he insists, he refused to quit.

He had known at the outset that he would face pain, hardships and many days of inclement weather.

He also knew that he would never give up.

Perhaps one of his most harrowing experiences occurred in November, when he and Orient had nearly achieved their goal of conquering the Appalachian Trail. Irwin lost his footing in a stream swollen by heavy rains, and he was dragged by the swift-moving current toward what he would later learn was a forty-foot waterfall.

Somehow, he managed to grab hold of a rock, and then, moving from rock to rock, he pulled himself out of the stream.

When Irwin and Orient finally reached the pathway's end in November, it had taken them eight exhausting and painful months to attain their goal of hiking the entire 2,144-mile length of the Appalachian Trail.

Their remarkable achievement marked the first time that a blind person had ever completed the trek, thus heralding yet another heroic effort that was accomplished through the mutually supportive partnership of a man and his dog.

How Far Can a Cat Fall and Survive?

Cats have begun falling from New York City windows and roofs in such unprecedented numbers that city veterinarians now refer in learned tones to the "high-rise syndrome in cats."

In a recent five-month period, 132 cats fell—or were pushed— from city windows. A remarkable 90 percent of the falling felines survived—including one which took a dive from a window on the thirty-second floor.

Research has determined that a cat can reach a terminal velocity of about sixty mph after free-falling about 130 feet in a few seconds. In actuality, the greater the distance a cat falls improves the animal's chances for survival. Of the twenty-two cats that the scientists documented had fallen eight or more stories, only one had died.

According to an extensive study, a cat falling a great distance will have more time to relax and to position itself for minimum injury. Cats appear to accomplish this by arching their backs, twisting their torsos independently of their hindlegs, and then bringing their hindquarters around. By thus spreading their limbs in a horizontal position, much like the position assumed by the so-called flying squirrels, cats are able to distribute the points of impact fairly evenly throughout their entire body.

By contrast, a falling human will reach a terminal velocity of 120 mph after plummeting for a few seconds, thus greatly limiting the height from which he or she can survive a collision with earth or concrete.

Mogadon Bounces off Bush to Survive Twenty-One-Story Fall

Mogadon, an eighteen-month-old black and white cat, was probably just enjoying a pleasant spring day in April 1993 when she was apparently startled by the voice of her owner's girlfriend telling her to get back into the apartment. The problem was, Mogadon was enjoying the fresh air and sunshine from a spot on a ledge that was twenty-one stories above the streets near Leeds, Alabama.

Claire Quickmire had only the kitty's best interests at heart when she attempted to call Mogadon inside, but the cat seemed to become confused. Perhaps she was used to taking such orders only from her owner, Mike Hawksworth.

In the next few seconds, the cat had fallen from her precarious perch and was plummeting toward the sidewalk below.

Claire recalled that the ride to the sidewalk in the high-rise's elevator was the longest elevator ride of her life. She fully expected to find Mike's kitty to be nothing more than a mangled mess of blood and fur.

She was astonished to find the dazed and frightened cat being comforted in the arms of a neighbor.

According to eye witnesses, Mogadon had streaked toward the cement, struck a bush at the side of the high-rise, then bounced onto the sidewalk. The befuddled cat picked itself up, then walked off, slightly dazed, but apparently not a great deal worse off than she was before the twenty-one story plunge to earth.

Claire gathered Mogadon into her arms and rushed her to a veterinarian, who found no broken bones, but who located numerous cuts and bruises to testify to the miracle survival. The supercat required twenty-four stitches, which seemed a very small price to pay for having endured an impossible fall.

Cat Survives Forty-Five Days Trapped Inside Bathroom Wall

After several days in her new home, Winnie Wagner of Orange Park, Florida, decided that either a cat was somehow trapped inside the wall near her bathtub or she had lost her mind.

Finally, in late February 1994, she had the marble paneling removed from around her tub, and a small cat blinked at them from inside the wall.

Winnie remembered that she felt faint when there was no longer any doubt that there really was a cat trapped inside the wall. She thought of all the nights that she had heard his pitiful cries—and all the while he was just inches away from her.

"Wally," as he was appropriately christened, was carefully removed from the bed that he had made of insulation, and Winnie took him to Briarcliff Animal Clinic in nearby Jacksonville.

Dr. Susan Ridinger weighed Wally in at only three and a half pounds, but stated that although dehydrated and weak, he was in "amazingly good shape, considering what he has been through."

The veterinarian theorized that Wally had lived off condensation from pipes under the tub in Winnie's bathroom, but doubted that the cat could have survived for much longer.

No one could venture any more than a guess as to how Wally had found himself trapped in the walls of the home, but educated estimates concluded that he had somehow managed to endure forty-five days sealed up in solitary confinement.

The story has a happy ending for Wally. More than 200 adoption offers for the amazing kitty flooded the clinic, and he was placed in a new home with a loving owner.

Two Weeks Without Food and Water in a Dresser Drawer

In the summer of 1993, drivers for Mollerup's Van and Storage Company in Roy, Utah, were puzzled by strange noises coming from some furniture pieces they were storing for a military family that was in the process of relocating.

Once they had pinpointed the peculiar sounds as issuing from a dresser, they opened a drawer to discover a female striped cat that resembled "a bag of bones."

Terri Anglen, of Mollerup's, declared the cat's survival an "absolute miracle." Her owners had been transferred to Hill Air Force Base in Utah from their present home in Michigan, and it was apparent that the cat had been trapped in that dresser drawer for two weeks without any food or water.

When the astonished owners of the cat were contacted, they said that they had searched high and low for their feline friend before their vanload of furniture had left Michigan for Utah. What had happened to their cat had been a complete mystery to them.

Terri Anglen said that the owners asked the cat's rescuers to be certain that she was fed and watered and loved until someone arrived to take her home.

Tiffany, Los Angeles' Symbol of Hope, Finally Lost Her Ninth Life

On March 3, 1994, forty-one days after the Northridge, California, earthquake, Tiffany, a ten-year-old Persian mix, was found alive in the closet in which she had sought sanctuary when the ground began to move under her feet on January 17.

Laurie Booth, Tiffany's owner, had searched everywhere for her beloved cat. She had posted signs, taken newspaper ads, asked her neighbors in Saugus if they could remember having seen the cat before or after the quake.

Ironically, Tiffany was only a few feet away from her desperate owner. Apparently, she had fled for safety to a neighbor's storage closet and had been accidentally locked in.

When she was finally found, Tiffany was dehydrated, nearly starved, and only fleetingly conscious. She had had no food for forty-one days and only a little rainwater.

Veterinarian Sandy Sanford, who treated Tiffany at the Animal Clinic of Santa Clarita, put her on intravenous vitamin, sugar and electrolyte solutions. Tiffany was fed orally every hour or so through a syringe because she was far too weak to feed herself.

"I still can't believe she's still alive," Laurie Booth told Rebecca Bryant of the Los Angeles *Times.* "When I picked her up she was just like a corpse. She was like a piece of tissue paper—frail and stiff and very cold."

Veterinarian John Burkhartsmeyer, owner of the Santa Clarita

clinic, expressed his opinion that Tiffany had "just barely made it
. . . Bones and skin is all that's left."

Tiffany's inspiring story of survival and will touched hearts as far
away as Europe. Veterinarians decreed her survival as "highly unusual, if not downright miraculous." Tiffany had become a symbol of
hope to all those citizens of California who sought to rebuild their
lives after the devastating effects of the quake of January 17.

On Friday, March 5, just as CBS News was at the Santa Clarita clinic
preparing to telecast a live report on Tiffany's fight for survival, the
valiant cat went into cardiac and respiratory arrest.

Veterinarian Sanford spent twenty minutes attempting to revive her
with cardiopulmonary resuscitation, oxygen and drug therapy, but
Tiffany, who had lost about 60 percent of her body weight during her
forty-one-day ordeal, was unable to respond.

Laurie Booth was distraught over her pet's death. How could she
not have heard Tiffany crying for her when she was so close in a
neighbor's storage closet? Why could she not have found her sooner
so that her life would have been saved?

But Laurie remained thankful that she had been able to find Tiffany when she was still alive: "She didn't die alone in a cold place.
She knew she was loved . . . She definitely was a little fighter."

CHARM, THE NEWFOUNDLAND MATCHMAKER

"My dog picked out the man I was supposed to marry," said Kim. Charm, Kim Pearce's Newfoundland 'matchmaker,' seemed to know they belonged together. Charm seems to say, "See, I told you so," as she lovingly looks to Kim and husband Scott for approval.

"Come on in—you belong here," Charm seems to be saying to Scott. When Kim, Charm's owner, saw the way her dog took Scott by the hand—she knew "he was the one!" *(Photo credit: Sherry Steiger)*

Adrien says that his dogs always seem to know when he is sad or upset about something. "I think they try to make me feel better— sometimes it works!" he says.

"I can tell when they are sad too," Adrien says as he pats Fisher on the head, telling him it's okay.
(Photo credit: Sherry Steiger)

Pictured here, the authors' dog, Simba, (deceased '90). Simba, a Lhasa-Apso who had apparently been trained by his previous owners never to bark in the house, saved all his barking up to share with the world when he would go outside to do his "duty." One time only he growled and barked ferociously. Even though he was nearly deaf from old age, he would not have been able to hear the other end of a phone conversation, had his hearing been perfect. He must have psychically picked up the authors' phone interview with a celebrity—the experience we were hearing about involved "demon dogs." Simba, who had been asleep in another room, shocked the authors as he came barking, hair standing on end and growling—at the phone! *(Photo credit: Sherry Steiger)*

Moses, the Steigers' Black Labrador, pictured here with Brad, has a special collection of toys that he keeps track of—and he always has one with him.   *(Photo credit: Sherry Steiger)*

Will Rogers once said to live your life like you were going to sell your parrot to the town gossip. That's good advice, but Rev. Wendell Hansen doesn't need to worry about his parrots embarrassing him. He's trained parrots such as these to sing, talk, ride miniature bicycles and do other tricks. With over thirty; that's right...thirty parrots of different varieties, he and his wife Eunice have a traveling Gospel Bird Show which has played in over thirty states!

(Photo credit: Sherry Steiger)

Maybe apes would make great pets. . . . if you have the room! The ape pictured here looks docile enough, although he would probably look less bored if he could watch TV with a human pal! Read about the French sailor's pet ape that was accused, tried and executed for being a "spy." *(Photo credit: Sherry Steiger)*

Believe it...or not—in 1499, a bear such as this one was taken to court for terrorizing German villages. The bear was given a death sentence. *(Photo credit: Sherry Steiger)*

How much do we really know about our pets? Pets have been known to travel across country to be with their owners. Is there such a thing as "destiny" between pets and their owners?

Moses was only five weeks old, too old to leave his mother, but he would not leave Sherry alone as she was looking around at a yard sale. Everywhere she went, Moses was on her feet. Was he meant to be the Steiger's dog? We think so. The bond has been magnetic between Moses, Sherry, daughter Melissa, (who trained Moses) and Brad. As Melissa snaps a picture of Mom washing Moses, he seems to be "saying" to her: "Oh yeah, how would you like your picture taken when you take a bath!"

Beatrice Leydecker has gained a growing reputation for her apparent
ability to communicate telepathically with animals. Pet owners
have been astonished by her seeming accuracy in determining an
animal's mental-emotional-physical problems and by her sensitivity
in relaying a pet's specific needs. In these two stills from the award-
winning documentary *Unknown Powers,* she mind-melds with a
troubled Dalmatian and a disgruntled goat.

(Photo credit: Unknown Powers, *winner of the Film Advisory Board's Award of Excellence
for 1978; a Don Como film, script by Como, Richard Kroy, and Brad Steiger.)*

Beatrice Leydecker with goat

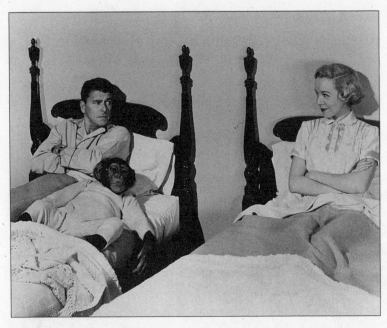

Many pets have made their owners and trainers very wealthy by becoming movie stars. Often they don't have to do as many "takes" to get the scene right as do their human counterparts. After his success in *Bedtime for Bonzo* (1951), Bonzo the chimpanzee went on to star in a sequel, *Bonzo Goes to College*—minus his costars Ronald Reagan and Diana Lynn.

Numerous dog owners have observed that their pooches really do not seem to mind wearing shirts, scarves, sweaters or hats. Maybe it makes them feel more human. Here, two well-coiffed canines are opening their very own Christmas presents.

Many people become so attached to their pets that, like Cathy Mulligan, they treat them like their own children. Here, Cathy is giving her dog, Little Mulligan, a cookie for his first birthday.

Patrick and Gael Crystal Flanagan and their beloved Pleiades. Pleiades, a unique vegetarian dog whose favorite treat is snow peas, saved the Flanagans' lives by alerting them to unseen danger while driving on a mountain road near Flagstaff, Arizona.

Stan Kalson states that his relationship with Lola taught him the true meaning of the power of love. Below, Lola in her sunhat against the Phoenix, Arizona, heat, makes a deposit at their bank.

Candy saw a black ghost cat on nearly a daily basis for months. The first time the cat appeared was under the dining room table. Candy would be watching television as she re-creates here.

(Photo credit: Sherry Steiger)

Candy Bossard saw a black ghost cat that appeared to her as real as this one. She soon found out why!

Besides being such wonderful companions to humans, pets can have friends too. These cats have been playmates for many years. Polka (white cat) is 13 years old, Rascal, (the dark cat) is 21 years old.

(Photo credit: Margaret Woodward)

Cats are renowned for picking up on people's energy fields. Pictured here, Sean, a cat belonging to Rev. Jon and Patricia Diegel, sprawls out on Rev. Diegel's foot as he performs a private wedding service for the authors. Nothing was going to keep Sean away—he had to be right in the center of the energy and the attention!

(Photo credit: Patricia Diegel)

Donkeys have become good friends to sheep and goats—and to the ranchers that raise them. They save ranchers millions of dollars a year by protecting their herds. Donkeys have a natural disliking for coyotes, wolves and dogs. Almost instantly the donkeys make friends with and start to protect the sheep or goats against their predators. In turn, the sheep and goats seem to understand the donkey's role of protector as they include the donkey as "family".

(Photo credit: Sherry Steiger)

"Beaky" the dolphin saved many lives. Deep sea diver Bob Holborn trained Beaky to be a lifeguard.   *(Photo credit: Sherry Steiger)*

SPACE AGE PETS

Genetic Engineering's House Pets of the Future

Perhaps in the future we won't be only watching whale shows at Marine Parks, or movies like "Free Willy". Genetic engineering may make it possible to have a pet dolphin or whale of your very own!
(Photo credit: Sherry Steiger)

Coming...going...
in between...or in
someone else's mouth?
Exotic pets could be in
style. Perhaps the alligator
or crocodile will be as
common as the pet turtle
or chameleon.

(Photo credit: Sherry Steiger)

Genetic engineering of the future would enable us to "miniaturize" huge animals, making it possible to have elephants and rhinos as exotic pets! *(Photo credit: Sherry Steiger)*

A face only a Mom could love!...Maybe if they were small, you could love a rhino for your very own pet! *(Photo credit: Sherry Steiger)*

Good neighbor Sam, the Pomeranian, poses for the camera.

Had it not been for Sam, Ken Bathaus might not have escaped this devastating fire.

Sam rescues his mistress and neighbor from a potentially fatal fire.

"Let's get out of here, we're not going to burn," Bessie says to her dog, Sam. Sam alerted his mistress to the flames shooting out of Bathaus' building next door.

Part Three

THE WEIRD SIDE OF ANIMAL-HUMAN RELATIONSHIPS

Kelsey Just Took the Car for an Innocent Little Spin

On a cold January day in Timmins, Ontario, it is certainly not uncommon for motorists to leave their automobile engines running while they dash quickly into a store to pick up a few items or into a private residence to say a brief hello to friends. And that was just what Valerie McNab did on a January day in 1994. The problem was, she left Kelsey, her Pomeranian-Chihuahua mix, alone in the car.

At some moment during the time that Valerie was chatting briefly with some friends, Kelsey apparently decided that driving a car had never looked all that difficult. He managed to slip the car into gear, and he took off on his joy ride through the streets of Timmins.

When Valerie bade her friends goodbye and came out to resume her errands in her car, she, of course, found that both the vehicle and her dog were no longer waiting for her.

She immediately called the police, who said that someone had just phoned in a report about having seen a car cross an intersection with a dog at the wheel.

Police officers drove Valerie a few blocks down the road, where they found her car stopped on the wrong side of the street. It was apparent that the car had struck a parked truck, but there was no real damage done to either vehicle.

When the officers approached Valerie's automobile, they found Kelsey fast asleep in the front seat, the very picture of complete innocence.

Motoring Mutt Takes Master's Jeep for a Joyride

It would seem that Brownie's driving ambition had always been to get behind the wheel of his master's Jeep and take it for a spin. And that's just what he did one fine summer's day in 1990 when his owner Russ Leigh stopped the vehicle and stepped out to talk to a friend.

With apparent confidence born of many hours of observing his master at the wheel, Brownie leaped behind the steering column, shifted the gear lever into reverse with his jaws, and hit the streets of Stockport.

Leigh, a garage manager, could not believe his senses when he saw his $15,000 Jeep careening out of control with Brownie at the wheel. The mutt had got into mischief before and got himself banished from the local McDonald's for stealing a hamburger out of a child's hands, but Leigh knew that this caper could be a much more costly one.

The Jeep traveled about fifty yards, smashed into a pickup truck, tore parts off both vehicles and kept on going.

Horrified by the infinite possibilities for damage suits with his dog driving hazardously through traffic, Russ Leigh set out on a run after the wayward Jeep.

He at last managed to catch up to the vehicle, jump behind the wheel, and put a screeching halt to Brownie's madcap machinations —just scant inches away from a shiny new Jaguar XJS.

Although the damage to his own vehicle and to the pickup cost him about £3,000, Russ Leigh said that he could never stay angry with Brownie. "When he's not getting into mischief," Leigh said, "he's a wonderful pet."

At the Time, It Seemed Like a Good Idea to Teach Tyrone How to Dial 911

Bonnie and Tom Robb of Aliso Viejo, California, had heard of noble dogs saving their owners by waking and rescuing them from fires and other home disasters, so, sometime in 1990, they decided that their highly intelligent cocker spaniel, Tyrone Jamal, could surely be trained to go those other heroic dogs one better and dial 911 as well.

Tyrone responded very well to the Robb's ingenious training program. They acquired a telephone with oversized push-buttons and dabbed peanut butter on the appropriate numbers. They would set off the smoke alarm, and Bonnie would scream and run to the bedside phone.

Tyrone enthusiastically joined in the fun and feigned excitement, and in practically no time at all he had learned to unhook the receiver with a swipe of his paw or a nudge of his nose.

Then one night the Robbs returned home to find the receiver off the hook. They thought little of it until the next month's bill included the charges for an adult dating service and a sports-pick hotline. That rascal Tyrone Jamal had obviously craved a little action while his owners were out for the evening, and he had run up a twenty-eight-dollar phone bill for his night's entertainment.

At first the telephone company was unsympathetic to the Robbs's incredible tale of a cocker spaniel who telephoned adult date lines, but when the crazy canine caper made headlines in the local newspaper, they agreed to remove the charges from the bill.

In the meantime, Tom and Bonnie bought a new telephone with buttons that Tyrone Jamal could not push—and put it out of his reach, just to be certain. "After all," the couple pointed out, "next time he could call Europe!"

The Ghost Dog That Smothered a Child

In May 1955, on the first weekend that the Frank Pell family spent in their new home on Coxwell Road in Birmingham, England, they were awakened by the sound of a slamming door.

Pell got out of bed to investigate, puzzled because he knew that he had carefully locked all the doors before retiring that evening.

As he stood in the kitchen, he heard a scraping sound like the noise a scrambling animal might make. It was as if an invisible dog were somehow scampering around him.

After a few moments of such eerie, unexplained sounds, the house was silent and Pell returned to bed.

As time passed, the Pells were visted nightly by an array of strange sounds. The greatest concentration of frightening noises occurred around midnight—and no matter how the doors had been secured, they banged to-and-fro, as if they possessed a will of their own. Eerie whispers of half-words and nearly understandable phrases echoed and swirled in the air around the Pells.

Both Frank and his wife knew that such things could have no natural explanation, and they lay awake nights, listening and wondering. Their dream house had begun transforming itself into a nightmare.

Once while cleaning the bedroom, Mrs. Pell felt a cold draft and what she later described as "icy, intangible fingers" running over her body.

Even though a sense of evil had clearly presented itself to the Pells, they resolved to do their best not to give in to it. Both of them were certain that fear of the unseen entities would only give the negative energy greater power over them. They reasoned that only those who feared supernatural forces could be harmed by them.

Then, one hot morning in June, the family awakened to the horror that their baby had suffocated during the night. The Pells's sorrow and sense of despair were only deepened by the fact that their child had been in the best of health and no mark of violence could be discerned anywhere on the infant's body.

Shortly after the child's burial, one of their sons startled them by asking if his baby brother had gone away with the little dog.

The Pells knew that no dog had ever entered the house, and they asked the boy when he had last seen the little dog.

"On the night the baby left us," their son replied. "The dog was sitting on the baby's face."

Mrs. Pell became hysterical, and Frank could not calm her. The thought that her baby had died from supernatural suffocation horrified her.

In an effort to exorcise the negative spirits in the house, they summoned a priest, but the religious ritual performed by the clergyman did nothing to quiet the disrespectful entities. The nocturnal bumping and banging continued with even greater regularity.

Then, on one of the first days of July, Frank Pell suddenly became conscious of foreboding whispers of greater volume than he had ever heard. The essence of evil became so strong that he feared for his wife.

He rushed to the stairs, where a frightening scene awaited him. His wife stood on the landing, transfixed with terror. Her limbs had stiffened and her hands clutched frantically at her side. The veins along her neck had swollen. Her eyes bulged with terror and her mouth gaped open in a silent scream.

When Pell ran up the stairs to help her, he ran directly into an invisible force that would not let him pass. It seemed to shroud him like a giant spider's web.

At last, with a powerful lunge, he was able to break through the unseen wall of evil—and at that instant, his wife's screams filled the house.

Without bothering to pack, the Pells took their children and left the house, resigning the place to the demonic dog and whatever monstrous thing owned it.

Later, friends of the Pells collected their belongings. They, too, heard the strange whispers, the weird thumpings, and the scratching and scampering of the invisible dog. Once they had finished packing, no inducement could bring them back into the accursed house.

Found: The Cheshire Cat's Smile!

Literary scholars and Lewis Carroll enthusiasts alike have long pondered the origin of the author's inspiration for Wonderland's Cheshire cat. From what source did he derive the bizarre feline that grinned at Alice until only its smile remained?

While most Carrollphiles have been willing to credit creative genius as the reservoir into which the author dipped his pen, others have been been quick to suggest that the toothsome cat with the lingering smile was first glimpsed by Carroll while in a drug-induced dream.

In July 1992, however, Joel Birenbaum discovered the original Cheshire cat lurking in the shadows at St. Peter's Church in Croft, Durham, England; and the longstanding mystery of where Lewis Carroll got the idea of a cat that disappeared leaving only a smile behind was solved at last.

One of thirty-five members of the Lewis Carroll Society visiting the church as part of a pilgrimage to various locations frequented by the revered author, Birenbaum observed a most curious phenomenon. As he knelt at the altar of St. Peter's, he noticed the image of a cat that had been crudely carved in relief on a stone wall panel.

As he knelt lower, he was astonished to perceive that the lighting in the tenth-century chapel created the illusion that the cat disappeared—except for its smile.

"When you look at the image of the cat from the front, it looks just like an ordinary cat," Birenbaum illustrated for his fellow Carroll enthusiasts. "But when you go down on your knees and look up, you can see only the grin and not the cat."

Carroll, whose birth name was Charles Lutwidge Dodgson, moved with his family from Cheshire to Croft when he was a boy of eleven. It seems likely, as Birenbaum has suggested, that the lad became intrigued by the illusion of the disappearing cat as he knelt in the chapel of St. Peter's Church. The peculiar effect apparently so delighted him that he used the lingering feline grin as an attribute of the Cheshire cat many years later in his famous *Alice in Wonderland.*

His Coonskin Hat Was Still Alive and Hissing

On the evening of August 12, 1993, Manchester, Iowa, police officers responded to a call regarding a domestic disturbance and found a forty-year-old male fighting with a female acquaintance outside of her home.

The man began to run away once he spotted the officers, but he was apprehended after a foot chase of less than a block.

Then, according to Police Chief Bruce Trapp, as one of the officers was putting handcuffs on the suspect, he saw eyes staring at him from on top of the suspect's head. "It began hissing and making other aggressive noises at the officer."

When the officer stepped back, he could see that the man's head-piece was a live raccoon. "It had ridden on [the suspect's] head all through the chase."

The raccoon was the suspect's pet, and it did not seem to like the police officer at all.

"The officer finally talked the suspect into calming the animal down," Chief Trapp said. "It was tame enough that he was able to walk it to his house."

The suspect was jailed on charges of assault, public intoxication, and interference with official acts.

Chief Trapp told Jack Hovelson of the Des Moines *Register* that no charges were filed against the raccoon. "He had no criminal intent."

Two Parrots Who Should Have Kept Their Beaks Shut!

While we must always behave responsibly toward our pets, there are times when we must also assume responsibility for their actions. Only the most passionate of parrot lovers would argue that the bird truly understands the content of the speech that it is mimicking. The person who teaches his parrot words and phrases must exercise common sense and a good measure of taste in selecting the items of speech that the bird will repeat.

In 1991, a soft-spoken, gentle-mannered sixty-eight-year-old woman was driven to suicide because she came to believe that her beloved Pete had turned on her and had become obscenely abusive toward her.

Nellie Smith, a retired nurse who lived in San Bernardino, California, bought Pete in a pet shop in 1989. Her family and friends were pleased that the sweet woman appeared to dote on the bird and to cherish its friendship. She had been widowed for many years, and it appeared to her children that Pete might provide an antidote for her loneliness.

A neighbor agreed: "Nellie loved that bird as if it were her child."

Then one day, according to a friend, Pete not only demanded his birdseed at once, he peppered his command with a string of four-letter words.

Nellie was visibly embarrassed, and she told the friend that Pete must have picked up the nasty language from watching television.

Shortly thereafter, Nellie hosted a dinner party for some of her friends, all of whom were used to approaching Pete and saying hello to him. The mild-mannered widow nearly had a heart attack when Pete answered each guest's greeting with a salty "F--- you!"

When the humiliated and confused Nellie stepped forward to silence and to shame Pete, he called her a fat cow and a portly pig.

From that night on, the parrot constantly heaped abuse upon the gentle woman. Friends heard the bird shout at Nellie to clean its cage. "Hurry, you stupid bitch!" it added with a nasty cackle.

One of her neighbors, shocked by the verbal abuse the parrot was heaping upon Nellie, urged the woman to get rid of the foul-mouthed fowl. "But she was too kind-hearted to give the bird away or to have it put to sleep. Maybe she thought Pete would stop insulting her and be his old self once again."

Tragically, Nellie finally snapped under the constant tirade of tart-tongued taunts that issued from the feathered fiend. Her suicide note asked her family's forgiveness for her desperate act, but stated strongly that Pete's incessant insults had turned her into a nervous wreck. "I'm sorry," she wrote, "but I just can't take it anymore."

Although Nellie remained convinced that her dear Pete had been corrupted by the foul language that he picked up from cable television, one of her neighbors believed that a prank-loving grandson had taught the parrot the obscene words and phrases "just to play a joke on his grandmother."

"If only Nellie had got rid of Pete, instead of herself," one of her friends said sadly.

In February 1991, a quarrel over a pet parrot led to one of the strangest trials in Norway's history. Frank Andresen claimed that the incessant babbling of Jokko, his next-door neighbor's fifty-year-old African gray parrot, had made his family's daily existence so miserable that his wife had suffered a heart attack.

Andresen's complaint stated that Jokko's constant chatter made it impossible for his family to read, to watch television, listen to the radio, or even to talk to one another. The opportunity to entertain guests in their home had become completely lost in Jokko's non-stop, nonsensical monologues. The crowning bombastic blow had occurred when Mrs. Andresen, so unnerved by the parrot's prattle, had suffered a heart attack and had to be hospitalized.

Jan Skog answered such charges by arguing that the only big mouth in the neighborhood belonged to Frank Andresen. Jokko, he insisted, was really a very quiet bird.

The four-day trial became a major Scandinavian media event. Skog maintained Jokko's innocence. Although he did come to admit that the parrot could imitate the roar of a moped's engine and sing a few bars of a Communist anthem, Skog insisted that Jokko did so "only rarely."

When Judge Sissel Hagen visited the Skog home to hear Jokko's repertoire for himself, the wise old bird sat in stony silence.

The unusual trial ended when Judge Hagen ordered Jokko kept away from the Andresens' side of Skog's home. And he admonished both Andresen and Skog to keep any future fuming, fussing and flapping parrot feathers out of his courtroom.

The Preacher Whose Birds Help Him Sing God's Praises

Rev. Wendell Hansen doesn't need to worry about his parrots embarrassing him with any nasty words, for he has trained his four macaws, four Amazon parrots, and two cockatiels to assist him in bringing biblical messages to audiences throughout the United States. And in addition to those ten feathered ministers of the Lord, Reverend Hansen has a backup crew of twenty other birds to help him spread the word.

The eighty-three-year-old Indiana minister has taught his birds to talk, sing, ride miniature bicycles, climb ladders, and perform a wide variety of other tricks—all of which are designed to deliver a message of inspiration.

Assisted by his son Dean and his wife Eunice on piano and organ, Reverend Hansen has brought his traveling gospel bird show to audiences in thirty states. A conventional minister in his youth, he hit upon the unique concept of using birds to win converts to the Lord.

Reverend Hansen may ask John, a yellow nape Amazon parrot, what he says when he goes to church. Without hesitation the parrot will squawk his reply: "Praise the Lord!"

When he has been complimented for stating the correct answer, John will sing out: "Hallelujah!"

Reverend Hansen said that he begins training the birds to speak his language when they are just babies, before they learn to communicate with "bird talk." And when they do it right, he added, "You give them a treat."

Having Trouble Getting a Credit Card?
Ask Your Pet to Get One for You!

Jim Kluczynski is a millionaire who owns a string of sandwich shops in Toronto. When he filled out an application for a Visa card in 1993, he really didn't foresee any problem in obtaining a piece of the precious plastic. When he was rejected, he was astonished.

Here he was, thirty-four years old, a successful entrepreneur with an estimated net worth of one million dollars. How hard must it be to get a Visa card?

Someone—Kluczynski swears he doesn't know who—overheard his complaint and thought it would be a good joke to fill out an application for a Visa card with another bank in the name of Mookie Kluczynski, Jim's pet cat.

Incredibly, almost by return mail, Mookie, a two-year-old black cat, got her Visa credit card. So Jim went out and bought some kitty litter on her new plastic passport to comfort.

Bank officials insist, however, that they did not extend credit to a cat, but to "Mr. Kluczynski, who has given the cat authority to use his account."

In early January 1994, retired Marine Corps sergeant Harold Calvert indulged a whim to see how easy it would be to get a credit card for his eight-year-old Brittany spaniel, Ginger.

He started sending in coupons and manufacturer's rebates in her name, and then in January Ginger received a preapproved gold MasterCard application. Calvert, sixty-nine, sent the form back "unsigned and unchanged."

A few weeks later, Ginger received her very own gold MasterCard with a $10,000 limit—double the limit of her owner.

Calvert said that now, when it is time to stock up on dog food and other pet supplies, they head for the mall with Ginger's MasterCard strung around her neck.

"To sign the bill," Calvert told writer Larry Masidlover, "I simply touch an ink pad to Ginger's paw, then touch the paw print to the sales slip."

Calvert said that the first bill had already arrived, but Ginger let him pay it with a check from his account.

The Horned Cat Creature That Sat at the Top of the Stairs

John Pendragon, the late British clairvoyant and seer, told us the following eerie account of a demonic ghost cat while we were collaborating on his biography [Pendragon—A Clairvoyant's Power of Prophecy, Award Books, New York; Tandem Books, London, 1968].

It was a very distressed Howard Leland who came to Pendragon on an October afternoon in 1943. Perhaps more than anything else, the man wished to receive validation of his supernatural experience and to be told that he was not going mad.

"I have been a volunteer with the A.R.P., the Air Raid Precautions, and a couple of nights ago during a raid, I took shelter in a deserted house in South London," Leland began his account of the frightening encounter. "I sat on the bottom step of the staircase, and after a few minutes I had the uncomfortable feeling that something was watching me from the top of the stairs.

"I clicked on my torch and flashed the beam upwards. I was startled half out of my wits to see a blackish brown, hairy creature that looked like an extremely large tabby cat squatting on the top stair—and the bloody thing had horns sticking out of its head!"

Leland paused to measure a distance from his forehead to indicate the approximate length of the protuberances. "And the monstrous thing had long, sharp-looking claws, too.

"The wretched beast and I stared at each other for fully half a minute," Leland continued his narrative. "I shall never forget the evil that shone in those eyes! I'm not ashamed to admit that I was too scared to either advance or retreat.

"Then the hellish cat thing, whatever it was, leaped from its squatting posture and seemed to jump into an empty room. I could hear it yowling and howling about."

At that point, Leland said, two pals of his entered the open front door. He explained as best he could what he had seen; and strangely enough, they did not laugh at him or start to give him the business about drinking on his watch.

"One of my mates told me that the hideous creature had been seen off and on in the neighborhood for years," Leland said. "Previous residents of the house had witnessed the thing. Always, it seems, the monstrous cat creature was seen sitting at the top of the stairs—in the very same spot that I had seen him."

At that point Pendragon interrupted him. "Did you or your friends go upstairs to look for any physical signs to corroborate your story?"

Leland nodded. He had felt more courageous in the company of his companions, and they had gone upstairs to investigate.

"We found not a thing," he admitted, shaking his head.

Then he narrowed his eyes and wagged a forefinger for emphasis, his voice rising to a near shout. "But I *did* see that monstrous creature on the stairs and no one can convince me otherwise! I am not subject to hallucinations—and I most certainly had not taken a drink that night."

Pendragon laughed softly. "There's no need to convince me. I shall be happy to take your word for your encounter."

"Then can you tell me what I saw, Mr. Pendragon?"

"What interests me," the clairvoyant said, "is *why* the creature was there. Please give me the address of the building."

Pendragon wrote down the address on a slip of paper and concentrated on it for several moments. No impression came.

He rose from his desk and stood before a large-scale map of

London that he had tacked to the wall. Looking closely at the map, he located the building in question—just a tiny dot amidst the thousands of dwellings in South London.

The moment Pendragon placed his forefinger on the miniscule dot, he suddenly "saw" the darkened stairway that was the lair of the hideous horned cat creature.

Something moved from the shadows. Not a creature, but a man. A despondent man who had sought to better his position in life by engaging in a practice of black magic, a smarmy endeavor that had included the ritual sacrifice of dozens of cats on his perverse satanic altar.

Pendragon's highly developed psychic abilities permitted him to view a most extraordinary recreation of a past event. Swirling about the devil worshipper as he walked toward the top of the stairs were the spirit forms of the many cats whose hearts had been ripped from their bodies by the cruel sacramental dagger. Pendragon reeled in a moment of vertigo as he felt the hatred of dozens of feline psyches focused on their murderer.

Then the clairvoyant noticed that the man carried with him a rope in which he had fashioned a noose. There was a brilliant flurry of macabre images, and Pendragon suddenly felt a violent constriction of his throat. Coughing spasmodically, he removed his forefinger from the map and reached for the cup of tea on his desk.

"If you will make inquiries," Pendragon told Leland after he had allowed the soothing tea to calm him, "I am certain that you will find that a previous resident of the house committed suicide by hanging himself from the banister at the top of the stairs."

"And the cat creature?" Leland wanted to know.

"Yes," Pendragon nodded. "It is there. It is quite likely an elemental spirit that has assumed the general form of the dozens of cats that this disturbed gentleman sacrificed on his satanic altar."

"An elemental?" Leland echoed. "And what's this about satanic rites and all?"

"A man hanged himself in utmost despondency when his attempt to better himself through the black arts failed," Pendragon explained. "This poor wretch had even resorted to animal sacrifice, slaying dozens of cats on his makeshift satanic altar. Elementals are prone to frequent places where a tragedy—generally suicide or murder—has occurred. They are also associated with places where black magic rites have been performed. They are most certainly a sort of personification of evil."

Pendragon recalled that Howard Leland returned to his office before the end of a week.

"I don't know how you managed to peg it," Leland told him, "but I learned from longtime residents in the neighborhood that a previous resident did indeed hang himself from a banister.

"Before the man killed himself," Leland continued, "folks said that they had been bothered by the sounds of cats yowling and screaming from the house in the middle of the night. And it was shortly after the man's suicide that people started seeing that terrible horned cat thing at the top of the stairs.

"I guess there really are more things between heaven and earth than are dreamt of in anyone's philosophy!" Leland concluded.

Her Little Cat Feet Held Diamonds for Her Mistress

"Ginny, you old silly! What have you got into now?" Mrs. Winifred Mansell of Keston, England, demanded of her pet cat, a large orange tabby. "You're limping, poor thing. Let's come to mother to have a look, eh?"

Mrs. Mansell had been taking full advantage of the lovely summer weather that early evening in 1955 to work in her garden. Ginny had been taking full advantage of her mistress' all-consuming concern for her flowers and plants and had gone off wandering in the nearby fields.

"Oh, darling," Mrs. Mansell exclaimed, the welfare of her beloved feline once again uppermost in her consciousness and the weeding of the flowers temporarily set aside. "You are limping badly. You must have picked up a nasty thorn in your paw."

When the woman lifted her tabby to examine its ailing left forepaw, she immediately spotted something shiny reflecting the fading light of early evening. Gently, she probed the paw with her right forefinger, but Ginny squirmed against the pain.

"Hold still now, love," Mrs. Mansell said, tightening her grip on the tabby.

As quickly as possible, she removed two particles that she at first believed to be chunks of glass from between the pads of Ginny's left forepaw.

But then, rubbing the tiny objects between the thumb and forefinger of her gloved left hand, Mrs. Mansell made a startling discovery: "They look like diamonds!"

The next morning Winifred Mansell was astonished to hear an experienced jeweler agree with her earlier analysis of the foreign objects that she had removed from the forepaw of her limping cat.

"Diamonds, madam," the jeweler pronounced. "Diamonds of rather good quality. Worth at least £300 each."

Somehow, somewhere, as she roamed the nearby fields, Ginny had managed to wedge two valuable diamonds between the pads of her left forepaw.

Had she dug up some miser's old unclaimed treasure trove? Had she somehow stepped on a burglar's hidden swag? Or had she just happened to have "found" diamonds that were lost during someone's stroll across the grassy fields?

No one ever determined the source of Ginny's mysterious booty, but Mrs. Mansell could proclaim that cats, as well as diamonds, are a girl's best friend.

Bizarre Court Cases of Animals on Trial—Terrible Perversions of the Human-Animal Psychic Bond

The deep, psychic bond that may exist between humans and their pets has never been more perverted than in those instances where legislators have carried anthropomorphism to its illogical extreme and decreed that animals should be prosecuted for their alleged misdeeds, just as if they had the reasoning capacity of humans. Some of the strange and bizarre trials that have been held have been justified by quoting Exodus 21:28: "If an ox gore a man or a woman that they die, then the ox shall surely be stoned."

Public Flogging for Pigs Found Guilty of Disorderly Conduct

In France during the Middle Ages, pigs could be punished for acts of disorderly conduct. They would be dressed in human clothing, then led into court for a trial.

If found guilty, they would be tied to a wheel and publicly flogged.

In the summer of 1457, the townspeople of Lavegny, France, even brought a judge from Paris to help judicate the charges of murder against a sow and her six piglets.

The prosecutor immediately announced that he would seek the death penalty for the sow that had killed a small child from the village.

The sow's defense attorney eloquently set forth a plea for justice. While there may have been no question of the sow's guilt, he argued, the pigs were of a tender age, relatively young, and under the influence of a mother who had set a bad example. They should be set free.

The trial lasted for more than a week, and the courtroom of spectators waited expectantly for the jury to return a verdict.

After several hours of deliberation, the jury announced its decision that the sow was, indeed, guilty of murdering the child. However, they recommended probation for the little pigs and admonished the local police to keep a close eye on them.

The courthouse square filled with townsfolk as the sow was brought from her cell to face the executioner. The hangman donned his dark robes, led the unfortunate sow to a gallows, and hanged her by the neck until she was dead.

The Bear Was Executed for Terrorizing German Villagers

In 1499, a bear was captured and brought to court after he had been terrorizing numerous German villages.

The massive marauder's attorney managed to win a slight delay in the beginning stages of the court proceedings when he made the point that the bear was not being judged by a jury of his peers.

The judge ruled that human jurors would be eligible, and the unfortunate bear was handed a death sentence.

A Large Gallows for a Very Large Bull

In 1516, a bull was held without bail in a French jail for goring a farmer. The jury decreed that the animal was guilty of premeditated murder, and the town was forced to construct a very large gallows to accommodate the official sentence that the bull be hanged.

The Hen Who Laid the Colored Egg Was Burned at the Stake

In 1471, a hen was arrested and taken to court in Basel, Switzerland, when she somehow managed to lay a brightly colored egg. Far from being pleased with such a unique addition to the hen's nest, the chicken's owner fearfully reported the event to church officials, who quickly concurred with his layman's analysis that the bird was possessed by a demon.

After a trial according to due process of law, the hen was found guilty of consorting with a demon and, together with other condemned witches, was burned at the stake.

Horses Were Liable for Riding Accidents

A horse was beheaded in 1639 for murdering a resident of Dijon, France, and a pony was hanged in Italy for throwing a woman rider and breaking her neck.

The Court Found the Field Mice Guilty of Eating Crops

During the sixteenth century, there was such a plague of field mice at Stelvio in the western Tyrol that the farmers, according to the custom in those days, charged the mice with a criminal offense—that of burrowing into the land and eating the crops.

The court gravely considered the case, and Hans Grienebner, a lawyer, was duly appointed to defend the rascally rodents.

His was not an easy task, but he solemnly pointed out that his clients did good as well as harm, for they ate numerous pests and fertilized the soil with their droppings. In his summation, he issued an impassioned plea that if the mice were not allowed to continue to live out the pattern of their natural lives, then he trusted that the court would be lenient with them.

The judge sentenced the mice to be banished from Stelvio, but in order that they should be protected on the journey, half a dozen soldiers were detailed to guard them on their way to the frontier. In addition, the compassionate judge decreed that any female mice who were pregnant or who had newly born infants would be granted a further fourteen days of grace before being forced to quit their homes.

It may be unnecessary to point out that the mice of Stelvio ignored the order of the court, so the local bishop was summoned and asked to pronounce a curse upon their furry heads. Although it is certain that the clergyman did his best to bring down fire and brimstone on the little beasties, the field mice remained utterly unmoved by his canonical eloquence.

The French Sailor's Pet Ape Was Executed for Espionage

In 1701, a French ship floundered in a storm off the coast of Dover, England, and was shattered against a reef. Before lifeboats could be launched, the crew had been sent to a watery grave. The only survivor of the wreck was a crewman's pet ape, who somehow managed to battle the rough sea and reached the shore.

The frightened, exhausted creature began to hunt for food, thereby startling the good citizens of Dover, who were quite unaccustomed to seeing an ape walking their streets. Urged to perform his duty by the townsfolk, a policeman arrested the ape and locked him up in the local jail to await the decision of the court concerning further disposition of the animal.

Since relations between England and France were strained—as they almost always were—the prosecutor felt that the case was quite clear-cut. Since the ape had come from a French ship, he must be, therefore, considered a Frenchman.

"There can be no question that the ape is a spy for the French army, which is likely planning an invasion of England," the prosecutor stated firmly. "This ape was all over town, quite obviously with the intent of spying on our defenses. He is clearly a spy."

The jury had to spend little time in deliberation. They quickly returned a verdict of guilt, and the ape was hanged for espionage.

The Magistrate Sentenced His Horse to Seven Years in Jail

In the early 1800s, Thomas Bainbrigge, a Nottinghamshire magistrate, struggled out of the muddy ditch into which his horse had thrown him and promised his untrustworthy steed a suitable punishment.

When he and his horse reached the stables at Bainbrigge's mansion, Woodseat in Sherwood Forest, he solemnly told his hands that the treacherous beast would be banished for life. But after he had washed and dined and mellowed himself with wine, he altered the sentence to seven years solitary confinement in jail—on short rations.

Beetles Banished from Berne for Missing the Trip on Noah's Ark

About the mid-1600s, the beetles in Berne, Switzerland, were given a court order to cease eating the farmers' crops and to leave the area at once. It seems that they, too, chose to ignore the judicial decree to quit the district, and in their case, the Bishop of Lausanne was asked to curse them.

The beetles had a most clever attorney, however, who charged the court that it would be very wicked of the bishop to pronounce a malediction upon creatures that Noah had taken with him into the ark. The peculiar case dragged on for nearly two years while the defense and the prosecution argued as to whether it was admissable for the beetles to be cursed.

At last the judge decided that the defense had been unable to present adequate evidence to prove that Noah had, indeed, taken a couple of beetles along with all the other paired creatures into the ark. The Bishop of Lausanne was summoned once again to bring his bell, book and candle and to administer a powerful curse against the disrespectful insects.

In this bizarre case, it was the clever bishop who gave the greatest demonstration of how to survive by one's wits. When, after several weeks, the beetles appeared to be ignoring his dreadful curse, the bishop thundered that the true fact of the matter was that God had visited the beetles upon the citizens of the district to punish them for their many sins.

Ants Condemned in Church Court for Invading Monastery

At Maranhão, Brazil, in the eighteenth century, a very strange event occurred, which appears to defy natural law. According to the official records, millions of pesky ants invaded the monastery of St. Anthony. The uninvited guests raided the stores of food, chewed away at various pieces of furniture, and had even begun to undermine the very structure of the building itself.

As for the monks, into whose habits and blankets the ants crept, their rituals became a riot, and their sacraments became scratching sessions. Their patron was, doubtless, St. Anthony, but his ants they did not cherish.

The bishop of the diocese, invoking the name of St. Anthony, ordered the ants to appear before an ecclesiastical court. According to the old records, the tiny felons obeyed the order in their millions.

A learned counsel defended them by pointing out to the clerics that his clients had been in possession of the land long before the monastery had been constructed; and by right of prior ownership, they were entitled to eat all that they might find on their domain. Pressing his advantage, the ants' attorney added that the monks were lazy, while the ants were industrious. It was a tactless statement, even if true; and it caused the ants to lose their case.

The bishop then commanded the ants to "begone to an area of barren land far distant from the abode of the brethren."

To the thankful delight of the monks and to the utter amazement of the common people, the ants—so the official records recount—"streamed forth in tens of thousands and marched in columns to the place assigned."

Weevils Ordered Out of St. Julien for Damaging Vineyards

In the seventeenth century, the weevils of St. Julien in Belgium, after having badly damaged some vineyards, were also ordered to be banished, but in their case the problem was to find them a suitable place to go.

A committee was appointed to seek a desirable area, and when it was found, a formal deed was drawn up assigning that particular tract of land to the weevils forever. As an afterthought, however, the committee insisted upon the addition of a clause that the good folk of St. Julien should retain mining rights.

The weevils' astute lawyer, Antoine Filliol, protested that his clients had no intention of inhabiting the aforesaid tract of land because it was well known that the troops of the Duke of Savoy were about to invade the province of the Marquis of Saluzzo, and they would most certainly march over the aforesaid tract of land, quite likely camp on it, thereby trespassing on the weevil reserve. Filliol stated that he was determined that his clients should not be trampled to death by hordes of common soldiers.

The plea by the weevils' defense lawyer resulted in the stay of execution of the sentence while the troops moved across the land in question.

When the invasion was over, the case against the weevils continued, and M. Filliol then argued that the soldiers had so damaged the land that it was no longer a fit place of residence for his clients.

How this intriguing case ended will probably never be known, for the remainder of the documents were destroyed.

Actually, they were eaten by weevils.

Dog on Bread and Water for Not Keeping His Teeth to Himself

In Libya in 1974, an overly aggressive dog was arrested after he had taken it upon himself to bite a man.

Found guilty after a trial, the malicious mutt was sentenced to be jailed for one month and to receive only bread and water.

Mary the Elephant Was Hanged for Murder

In September 1916 in Kingsport, Tennessee, a new handler, twenty-three-year-old Red Eldridge, was helping to steer the circus elephants on a predetermined parade route through town.

As the regal pachyderms plodded through the Kingsport streets, Mary, a massive queen elephant, spotted half a watermelon that someone had left on a curb. Apparently delighted at the prospect of such a tasty and succulent treat on that warm September day, Mary uncoiled her trunk and swung it toward the discarded melon.

Young Eldridge, conscientiously performing the instructions of the task assigned to him in his new position, sought to prod Mary back in line with a stick.

Massive Mary, however, was not in the mood to be corrected or to be told that she could not indulge in that tasty melon. She grabbed Eldridge with her powerful trunk, lifted him over her head, and hurled him violently against a nearby refreshment stand.

While the ladies in the crowd screamed, the children cried, and everyone scattered and ran for cover, the young trainer lay sprawled unconscious.

Mary was not finished with the new trainer who had sought to thwart her wishes. She moved her great bulk over to where he lay dazed, lifted a giant foot into the air, and brought it down hard to flatten Red Eldridge's head.

A pistol appeared in a bystander's hand, and he shot Mary five times.

When the bullets appeared to have no effect on the behemoth, the crowd began to rally and to chant, "Let's kill the elephant!"

A circus official pushed his way through the vengeful mob, managed to calm them, and walked the wounded elephant back to the circus grounds.

Incredibly, Mary performed her act under the big top that night with all five bullets in her tough hide.

But before the performance had ended, a rumor had circulated throughout the audience that young Red Eldridge had been Murderous Mary's sixteenth victim.

When the circus moved to Erwin, Tennessee, the next day, an angry mob demanding justice met them at the railroad yard and forced the circus officials to agree that the killer elephant should be sentenced to death.

A chain was fastened around Mary's mammoth neck and attached to a huge wrecking derrick. She was hoisted six feet into the air to be hanged by the neck until dead, but her several tons of weight soon snapped the chain.

The condemned elephant fell to the ground, and the crowd ran for cover, fearing that the giant would go on a foot-stomping rampage and seek other bodies and heads to flatten.

But the confused Mary was dazed senseless and offered no resistance when railroad workers looped a steel cable around her neck.

Once again the derrick pulled away at the elephant's great bulk and began to hoist her into the air. This time the cable held.

According to eyewitnesses of the weird execution: "Murderous Mary kicked a little, then went limp. She had met her end. She was dead."

Phantom, the Canine Sheep Rustler

Sadly, some pets can be made to follow a life of crime. And sometimes they become better at pursuing criminal activities than their human teachers.

In 1960, James McKenzie of North Orago, New Zealand, thought he was being exceedingly clever when he taught Phantom, his collie, how to rustle sheep.

Everything went McKenzie's way for a while. He would watch gleefully from a safe hiding place while Phantom skillfully cut several hundred sheep out of a rancher's herd and guided them away to the pens that were awaiting the stolen woolies.

Eventually, though, McKenzie's schemes were dashed by angry ranchers and effective police surveillance. McKenzie went to prison for five years—but Phantom managed to get away and was never caught.

The Incredible Things That Dogs Will Try To Eat!

Tyro, a twenty-pound Labrador-Newfoundland-mix puppy, began acting listless and started to vomit, but his owner, Valerie Faulkner of Richmond, British Columbia, did not think too much of it until his symptoms continued into the second day.

A trip to veterinarian Dr. Cliff Hatfield and his X-ray machine revealed a nine-inch carving knife in Tyro's tummy. Emergency surgery removed the knife, which, luckily, had been swallowed handle first.

In January 1994, it took veterinarian Elaine Caplan of the New York Animal Medical Center two hours to remove a twelve-inch cake knife from Apple's stomach. Apparently, while the nine-month-old Border collie's owner, Eric Fuchs, was out playing cards for the night, the hungry dog gulped down a hefty slice of devil's food cake—along with the cake knife.

Fred Lundberg, who owns the Woodcutter's pub in Dorset, England, had to rush Eric, his Great Dane, to the vet's during a recent pool tournament being held in his bar. It seems that right in the midst of a tense match, Eric leaned over the pool table and swallowed the cue ball!

Art Pelz, of Creative Jewelers in Laguna Beach, California, was nonplused when his guard dog Duque suddenly jumped up and swallowed the $15,000 diamond ring that he had been cleaning for a customer. The sixty-pound pooch was rushed to veterinarian Dr. James Levin, who extricated the ring from Duque's stomach with some medicine that made the dog vomit.

Genetic Engineering's Amazing House Pets of the Future

In November 1986, journalist Larry Haley asked a number of futurists, ourselves included, to theorize regarding the future of pets, if genetic engineering should develop to the extent that some scientists suggest.

Dr. William Hanson, professor of biology at California State University, speculated that in the early years of the twenty-first century, ". . . we may well see the creation of the first minianimal. We have the technology to manipulate animal species."

Joining the speculative projections, we foresaw minipets that might include twelve-inch elephants, lions and tigers the size of house cats, and eight-inch whales for the home aquarium.

Continuing our predictions, we stated that such minipets ". . . will be inexpensive, costing less than one of today's pedigreed poodles. They'll be easy to care for, obedient, and much less likely to need veterinary care than today's house pets."

Dr. Hanson added: "Their inherent ferocity will be reduced or even eliminated."

Dr. Thomas Easton, a theoretical biologist and futurist agreed with such speculations: "The technology exists today through experimental genetic engineering. Scientists are currently able to transplant genes, the biological blueprints that tell the animal how to design and make its various body parts."

When asked for more ideas of what kinds of pets a household may aspire to in the future, we answered thusly: "Gorillas the size of Barbie dolls will give new meaning to the phrase, 'More fun than a barrel of monkeys.'

"Eagles and falcons the size of parakeets will be bred with the intelligence and instincts of homing pigeons. Hippos the size of hamsters will provide a real incentive to lure your three-year-old child into the bathtub.

"And none of these minipets will be vicious, cruel or destructive. You'll never have to be concerned about these miniature lions or tigers clawing up the furniture."

Nuclear Accidents Can Create Monstrous Pets

While it may be amusing to speculate about the kinds of pets that might be created through genetic engineering in our future, it is frightening to consider what horrible things can be worked on unsuspecting animals through nuclear radiation.

If we had heard the following report only once or twice, we would be inclined to dismiss it as unfounded rumor. And even though we cannot swear to the report's complete authenticity until Russian scientists step forward to verify the accounts, it would seem that the awful accident that occurred at the Chernobyl nuclear plant in 1986 created monstrous animals as a part of its ghastly byproduct.

Certain conscientious Russian and Ukrainian scientists have already testified to the creation of giant pigs, twice their normal size, some with three eyes and mouths like frogs. Others list eight-legged horses, two-headed cattle and birds.

Numerous scientists have accused the former Soviet government of having launched a massive coverup of the events surrounding the Chernobyl nuclear disaster, and they are demanding a cleanup campaign of the "forbidden zone," which some scientific investigators state was at one time 1,000 times higher than normal radiation counts.

Igor Sklarevsky, writing in the influential Russian newspaper *Literaturnaya Gazeta,* reported in detail on the Chernobyl monsters, including dogs and cats that have grown to three times their normal size. Sklarevsky insists that people know these monstrous creatures exist because nomads and hunters constantly venture into the forbidden zone and return with stories of horrendous mutated animal monsters.

Part Four

PETS IN THE SPOTLIGHT: THE CELEBRITIES AND THE INHERITORS

Strongheart, First of the Hollywood Wonder Dogs

Many legendary animal actors are immortalized in concrete at the superposh Burbank Animal Shelter's "Paws of Fame." Visitors to the shelter are able to see the paw, claw, and hoofprints of such big-screen names as Old Yeller, Lassie, Benji and Mr. Ed.

Among the earliest lessons that Hollywood film makers learned—'way back in the days of silent films—was that audiences loved to see animals perform in motion pictures.

Mack Sennett, who created all those zany slapstick comedies starring Charlie Chaplin, Ben Turpin or the Keystone Kops, supported his human comics with Pepper the cat, Butterfly the horse, and Teddy the dog.

For the most part, the roles of animals in the movies—and in other aspects of celebrity—have been those of supporting players to the human actors or to their owners. On numerous occasions, however, animals have managed to achieve a star status of their own.

Strongheart, a German shepherd whose real name was Etzel von Oeringen, became the first animal star in the movies. "Etzel," who first starred in *The Silent Call* in 1921, may have been one of the most intelligent dogs on record—in or out of the movies. A number of his almost preternatural feats are featured in the inspirational book *A Kinship with All Life,* written by J. Allen Boone, the movie producer and former head of RKO studios.

Boone stated that when he first acquired the international champion German shepherd, he was told to interact with the dog as if he were an intelligent human being. He was advised to say nothing that was not truly in his heart, and it was suggested that he read something of value to Strongheart each day.

Because the open-minded movie producer took such advice seriously and permitted himself to treat the dog with respect, he was treated to many instances in which he could actually observe Strongheart's ability to solve numerous problems in an intelligent manner. Boone freely admitted that, prior to his experiences with

141

Strongheart, he had been taught that qualities of reason and judgment "belonged more or less exclusively to the 'educated members' of our species."

On the first night that Boone had Strongheart as his house guest, he decided that it would be all right for the famous German shepherd to sleep with him in his double bed.

Boone became quite annoyed when Strongheart insisted on lying with his head pointing towards the foot of the bed. This meant that his rear end was on the pillow. No matter how famous this dog was, Boone didn't care for having to sleep next to Strongheart's rear end!

Boone finally ordered the dog to sleep with his head pointing towards the bed's head like he himself was doing. Recounting Boone's description of the dog's reaction to his charge:

> *"Strongheart suddenly moved forward, closed his jaws on one of my pajama sleeves and tugged me gently but firmly to the foot of the bed. A short distance away were some rather insecure old French windows covered by long curtains. Getting an end of one of these in his teeth, Strongheart pulled it back, held it there for a few seconds and then let it drop back into position again. Then he began barking, swinging his head rhythmically back and forth between the French windows and me.*
>
> *"Had he spoken in perfect English, he could not have told me more clearly what he wanted me to know: that whenever he lay down to relax either temporarily or for his night's sleep, he always wanted to have the front end of himself—his eyes, nose, ears and jaws—aimed in the direction of possible danger. If trouble did enter in human form, he could go into action without having to lose time by turning around. And those old French windows were certainly a possible trouble entrance."*

Boone and Strongheart compromised by turning the bed around so that they could both lie with their heads in the direction of the suspicious windows.

In *A Kinship with All Life,* Boone wrote, "For the first time, I was actually conscious of being in rational correspondence with an animal. I had been privileged to watch an animal acting upon its own initiative put into expression qualities of independent thinking, clear reasoning, good judgment, foresight, prudence, and common sense."

Canine Stars of the Silver Screen

Rin Tin Tin was another German shepherd superstar who gained a large mass following. "Rinny" may not have been quite as intelligent as Strongheart, but he singlehandedly kept the Warner Brothers studio afloat until the talkies were introduced in 1927.

The "Little Rascals" of Hal Roach's *Our Gang* short comedies, largely produced in the 1930s, continue to win new fans through the process of perpetual rebirth known as television syndication. While we remember Spanky, Alfalfa and Buckwheat, we also cherish the memory of their faithful dog Pete with the black ring around his eye.

Lassie, who was really a male dog named Pal, eclipsed Strongheart and Rin Tin Tin in mass popularity when the classic film *Lassie Come Home* was released in 1943. A series of MGM motion pictures made "Lassie" and "collie" virtually synonymous, and Lassie continued "her" career with a successful television series.

"Lassie" is about to return to the big screen in a Lorne Michaels production. The new Lassie is male, as was each of the previous ten incarnations of the classic collie hero. Female canine actors are at a disadvantage if they aren't neutered, because they go into heat twice a year.

Bob Weatherwax, son of Rudd, the trainer who launched the Lassie dynasty in the 1940s, said that "Lassie" went on to star in nine movies and 400 television episodes. During the course of the television series, Lassie won two Emmys.

"As long as there are children, there will be a Lassie," Weatherwax said.

*   *   *

On the other hand, Benji, whose series of movies rake in millions of dollars [*Benji the Hunted* made $22 million in the summer of 1986], is a twelve-year-old *female*. Writer-director Joe Camp noted that Benji started her first movie when she was only eleven months old: "She had a whole movie on her back when most dogs are playing with puppy toys."

For seven years, she was the cute little mutt named Higgins who played a supporting role to the cute big girls on the TV series *Petticoat Junction*. The lovable, mangy little female mutt had been discovered by trainer Frank Inn at the Burbank Animal Shelter, and he transformed the dog into one of Hollywood's hottest animal stars.

In 1974, Higgins changed her name to Benji, and she became the star of a series of very successful movies. Via the magic tricks of Hollywood, just as Lassie is really played by a male dog, Benji is actually a female dog.

One of the biggest hits of the summer of '92 was the comedy that featured a mammoth St. Bernard named Beethoven, his loving human family, and the harried father, played by Charles Grodin.

Chris was Beethoven's birth name, but since the first film grossed $150 million worldwide, everyone now addresses him by his professional name. While working on *Beethoven's 2nd*, executive producer Ivan Reitman said that, once the big St. Bernard believed that he had done a scene correctly, it was very hard to convince him to do a second take. Success has granted Beethoven his own air-conditioned trailer on the set.

Television Goes to the Dogs

The cast of television's *Empty Nest*, including Richard Mulligan, David Leisure and Dinah Manoff, laughingly admit that Dreyfuss is the big star of the show. Dreyfuss's real name is Bear, and he has more than twenty tricks in his repertoire, including shaking hands, opening doors, raising his eyebrows—and slobbering on cue.

Animal trainer Bill Berloni, who groomed an Airedale for superstardom as Sandy in the Broadway blockbuster musical *Annie,* not long ago plucked Riley, a spunky, two-year-old wire-haired terrier, to play Asta in the musical version of *The Thin Man.*

And a few years ago, who could have overlooked the everywhere-present countenance of Spuds MacKenzie, the black-eyed bull terrier that a beer company tried to make us believe was the "Guru of Good Times" or "The Philosopher of Fun"? Merchandising gimmicks for Spuds (rumors circulated that the King of Party Time was really a girl bull terrier named Evie) reached the incredible total of some 200 items, including Spuds coffee mugs, posters and T-shirts.

When Spuds passed to Doggy Heaven in 1993 at the age of ten, it was finally revealed that he was a she—Honey Tree Evil Eye, by name.

Bob Lachky, Bud Light marketing director at Anheuser-Busch, commented that Spuds had been the "booster rocket" to the brand's success. "It truly was one of the most powerful advertising ideas in the last twenty-five years."

Moose, the three-year-old Jack Russell terrier who plays Eddie on the 1993–94 television season's comedy hit *Frasier,* has become such a popular member of the cast that he receives hundreds of pieces of fan mail each week. Moose's trainer, Mathilde De Cagny of Birds & Animals Unlimited, noted that the dog had spent his early years as a common house dog whose original owner had put him up for adoption. Kelsey Grammer, the star of the show, pronounces Moose a true professional and a joy to work with.

Maui is the five-year-old collie-mix who plays Murray on the hit Paul Reiser-Helen Hunt comedy *Mad About You.* His trainer Betty Linn complains that success has "completely spoiled him." As soon as people start arriving on the set, she says, everybody starts petting him.

* * *

Cody, who plays a wolf on the popular drama *Dr. Quinn, Medicine Woman,* is actually a malamute dog. Dennis Grisco, his trainer, confides that the ten-year-old dog is in love with actor Joe Lando, who plays mountain man Byron Sully on the series. Although he is supposed to be a fierce wolf, Cody is actually such a pussycat that he has a stand-in named Mika brought in for all the snarling scenes.

At age eleven, Samantha, who plays Earnest on *Dave's World,* is one of the oldest active animal performers in the business. Although she has those droopy, lazy hound-dog eyes, Samantha was a rescue dog for eight years before her debut in the 1993 motion picture *Amos & Andrew.*

Riding the Hollywood Range

While dogs may enjoy the lion's share of animal starring parts, they by no means have a monopoly on roles that win audiences' hearts. For example, what teenager—especially the girls, it seems—could not fall in love with such sturdy stars as the horses Fury, Flicka and the Black Stallion?

And, of course, we cannot forget Francis, the talking mule, and Mr. Ed, the talking horse, for a little comic relief.

Neither can we pass by all those cowboy stars with their faithful, four-legged partners. How far would old-time range rider Ken Maynard have got without his horse Tarzan?

Tom Mix, the superstar of the silent screen, could never have rid the West of outlaws without Tony.

Gene Autry's songs just wouldn't have sounded quite as good if he hadn't sung most of them on the back of Champion.

And no matter how stalwart he might have been, Roy Rogers could never have beaten off the bad guys and won Dale Evans's heart without his marvelous palomino stallion Trigger. (His trusty German shepherd Bullet did his share to chew up the villains, as well.)

Feline Stars Also Light Up the Motion Picture Screen

Rhubarb was a pretty big cat star; and Clarence the Cross-Eyed Lion was a very big "cat" in size, but the incredible Syn Cat was declared by animal trainer Al Koehler to be ". . . the smartest, most sociable, most emotionally stable cat in the world."

Proclaiming Syn Cat, the affable Siamese, to be a feline that only comes around once in a lifetime, Koehler saw Syn Cat go on to star in such memorable Disney films as *That Darn Cat* and *Incredible Journey.*

And before there was the finicky Morris hustling catfood in all those television commercials, there was the elegant and stylish Nicodemus, who lived a true ugly duckling story. The unwanted runt of a pedigreed litter, Nicky grew to be the glamorous, snowy white Persian who became a famous model for Revlon cosmetics. Nicodemus, in fact, went on to become a cottage industry; and the sophisticated cat even guested on the *Today Show, Captain Kangaroo, Play Your Hunch,* and many other television shows.

The Real-Life Inspirations for the Pets on the Comic Pages

Cartoonist Brad Anderson, creator of Marmaduke, the lovable brute of a Great Dane, admitted that the dog in the comic strip is modeled after his mother's dog, Bruno, a boxer. When he created the strip in 1954, he decided to make his character a Great Dane, figuring the bigger the breed the better—and the more comical. Now Anderson

and his wife have their own Great Dane, Marmaladee, a gift from
their daughter Christine.

George Gately received his inspiration for the pugilistic cartoon
pussy Heathcliff from his brother's tough, independent tabby, Sandy.
"All the dogs in the neighborhood were afraid of him," Gately re-
calls. "Sandy would fight anything on four legs—a lot like Heathcliff."

Garfield's creator, Jim Davis, had twenty-five cats when he was a
kid, but doesn't have one now because his wife is allergic to them.
The cartoon cat is based on a variety of his friends' cats, Davis said.
"I grew up on a farm and cats were all over the place. The fact that I
don't have one now means I use other people's cat stories and
Garfield is more of a general kind of cat."

Pets in the White House

Franklin D. Roosevelt, Richard Nixon, Lyndon Johnson—and practically every United States president back to Andrew Jackson—have
made a pretty big thing about their canine companions. And now we
have a White House cat in the august, furry body of Socks, the pet of
the Clinton family. We can but wonder if Socks will follow the example of Millie, former first lady Barbara Bush's dog, who actually
wrote her own book about life in the White House.

As it turns out, Mrs. Bush and Millie were really very close. In fact,
they are sisters in suffering. Barbara takes the steroid prednisone to
battle Graves' disease, a thyroid condition, and Millie takes the same
medication to battle lupus, an inflammatory disease. What is more,
they both suffer the identical side effects—weight gain.

Socks Is Not the First White House Cat

Although our nation's first president, George Washington, had a number of cats with such names as Truelove, Sweetlips, Mopsy and Madam Moose, none of them made it to the White House for the simple reason that the presidential residence was not ready for occupancy until 1800, three years after Washington completed his last term in office.

Abraham Lincoln's son Willy owned a cat who soon gave birth to a whole litter of kittens that the president took great delight in helping to name. According to available historical records, the Lincoln litter [*circa* 1862] constitutes the first cats in the White House.

When Rutherford B. Hayes was in the presidential residence from 1877–81, his gift of a Siamese cat from the U.S. consul in Thailand was the first of that breed in the country.

President Theodore Roosevelt, who is usually associated with big game animals, nonetheless had a six-toed cat named Slippers, who enjoyed a run of the White House from 1901–09. More in keeping with his rugged reputation, Teddy also at various times gave presidential refuge to a bear, a lizard and a snake.

Woodrow Wilson, the tireless champion of world unity who won the Nobel Peace Prize in 1918, tried his best to break his cat Puffins of his penchant for chasing birds. According to the story, one day what appeared to be an entire flock of birds swooped down on the feline predator and gave him such a good pecking that he never bothered another bird from that time on.

Silent Cal Coolidge proved during his time in office from 1923–29 that he was not such a dour fellow after all, when people saw the affection that he displayed for his cat Tiger. Once when the cat wandered off, Coolidge took advantage of his office to prevail on all the Washington, D.C. radio stations to put out all-points bulletins to locate Tiger. Fortunately for cat lover Cal, Tiger was found and returned to the White House.

In addition to Tiger, Cal's favorite, the Coolidge family kept a number of other cats, an aviary of birds, numerous dogs and a raccoon named Rebecca that Mrs. Coolidge liked to walk on a leash.

President Bill Clinton has often expressed his admiration for President John F. Kennedy, and it seems that he also shares JFK's allergy to cats. While little Caroline Kennedy, like Chelsea Clinton, did own a cat, her Tom Kitten was sent off to live with the first lady's press secretary. Caroline continued her long-distance relationship with Tom Kitten for years and came to visit his grave and pay her respects after he died.

Pets and Their Celebrity Owners

And what about the pets of show business celebrities?

NBC *Tonight* host Jay Leno had to return to his former residence at 3:30 in the morning on moving day to appease the tearful demands of his cat-enthusiast wife Mavis, who would not go to bed until the body of her late beloved cat was reburied in the lawn of their new home.

The Golden Girls star Betty White supports three pooches, Dinah, Cricket and Timmy. Ms. White's fellow "Golden Girl," Rue McClanahan loves cats so much that her house is overrun with them, and she has even shared her advice for cat owners on *The Cat Care Video Guide.*

Model-actress Brooke Shields fancies dogs, while soap star *[The Bold and the Beautiful]* Katherine Kelly Lang is devoted to horses.

When Vanna White isn't turning letters on *Wheel of Fortune,* she may well be teaching the vowels to her cats, Ashley and Rhett Butler. "I can have a very bad day," she said, "but just being in the presence of my little precious ones makes me feel better. Cats are very affectionate and giving, if you treat them with love. They have certainly enchanced my life."

Talk show host Sally Jessy Raphael no doubt agrees with Vanna White that cats may provide an emotional uplift, and she probably finds it quite relaxing that her blue-eyed cat Sheba never talks back to her around the house.

Seventy-year-old Aurelia Schwarzenegger, Arnold's mom, is honorary president of Noah's Ark House, which wages a war against animal cruelty in her hometown of Graz, Austria. Mrs. Schwarzenegger is devoted to collecting stray cats and dogs and keeping them away from those who might terminate them.

Kim Novak, once touted as Marilyn Monroe's chief competition in Hollywood, retired from the screen years ago to devote herself to the care of animals. Ms. Novak followed the example of one of filmdom's brightest stars, actress-singer Doris Day, who left the silver screen to form the Doris Day Pet Foundation, an organization dedicated to helping animals that are hungry, homeless or hurt.

Certainly one of the most active of all show business celebrities who devote their time to the welfare of animals, Doris Day not only cares for her regular family of four-legged friends who share her eleven acre estate near Carmel, California, but she has set up special 800 telephone numbers for people who have either lost or found pets during such disasters as hurricanes, floods and earthquakes.

"My life has been made so full, thanks to all my pets," she said recently. "Animals are the best things on earth. Sometimes they're even better friends than humans."

People interested in adopting one of the homeless pets rescued by her foundation may write directly to the Doris Day Pet Foundation, PO Box 8166, Universal City, CA 91608.

Bob Barker announced that he would refuse to host the Miss U.S.A. contest in 1988 because fur coats were being given to the contestants. The genial *Price Is Right* host has been speaking up for abused animals since 1979, and his support of the United Activists for Animal Rights has helped to make the organization become a powerful force for the humane treatment of animals.

Actors and Others for Animals was created as a nonprofit group in North Hollywood in 1971 by the distinguished actor Richard Basehart and his wife Diana. Earl Holliman *[Delta]* is the current president and Jo Anne Worley *[Laugh-In]* and Loretta Swit *[M*A*S*H]* are among the group's directors.

Pet Tortoise Inherits Spinster's Estate

If Fred the tortoise should ever be challenged to a race by an arrogant and speedily confident hare, he can simply summon his chauffeur to drive him across the finish line.

Although British spinster Dolly Duffin left only a few hundred pounds to a niece, her nearest living relative, she bequeathed approximately £65,000 to old Fred, her beloved tortoise.

Precisely how one becomes so attached to a tortoise may seem difficult to define, and Dolly's niece Susan Kirkwood is probably at a greater loss to explain her aunt's love connection to Fred than is anyone else. Mrs. Kirkwood admitted that she had anticipated receiving a sizable inheritance from her aunt's estate, explaining that Dolly had once promised her the money.

Before the sixty-one-year-old spinster died in March 1990, she was seen carrying the hefty tortoise on her shoulder, as one might hold a child. Dolly was even observed walking Fred in a baby carriage.

According to the terms set forth in her will, Dolly's house was bequeathed to the Humane Society with clear instructions that it was to be sold and that all proceeds of the sale should go to the care and keeping of Fred for the rest of his natural life—which could well be another sixty years or more.

Mrs. Kirkwood was philosophical about her aunt's decision to leave the great bulk of her estate to a tortoise. "What we never had, we will not miss."

Half a Million Dollars to Provide Pets for Senior Citizens

When former University of Wisconsin professor Dwan T. Wick of Hokah, Minnesota, died in December 1993 at the age of seventy-one, he left no spouse, no children, and no brothers or sisters. His companion, when he left the earthly world behind him, was a cat.

According to Wick's attorney, Ross Phelps, the professor said that he liked the work of the Purina Pets for People program in St. Louis, so he decided to bequeath $545,000 to their goals of providing pets for senior citizens.

A Hearty Christmas Dinner for Homeless Dogs

During the holiday season of 1993, British retiree Leslie David left $90,000 to the canine residents of a Birmingham, England, dog's home, asking that the sum be used to prepare them tasty turkey dinners for Christmas.

Nickie and Carla Live Alone in a $100,000 House

Before Helen Walsh died in 1987 at the age of eighty, she made certain that her two canine companions Nickie and Carla would be able to remain in her Memphis, Tennessee, home until their natural deaths. In addition, she saw to it that there would be ample finances set aside to provide food and veterinary care for as long as they lived.

Sister Mary Michael Greaber, a niece of Helen Walsh, stops by twice a day to walk the dogs, feed them, and to turn the color television set on and off.

Sister Mary told writer Peter Fenton that all the folks in the neighborhood had great affection for Nickie and Carla, and no one begrudged them their good fortune. "They're the two most lovable pets in the world. They gave Aunt Helen so much happiness that she couldn't bear to think of them alone and miserable after she passed away."

According to Sister Mary, the $100,000 house will be sold after the two dogs have passed on, and the money will go to charity.

The World's Richest Pet Lives on His Estate Near Pisa, Italy

Gunther IV, a one-year-old German shepherd, has the grand sum of $80 million at his disposal, thus making him the richest pet in the world.

And talk about a dog's life! Gunther has nothing to do all day but take an occasional dip in his custom-built pool or to relax in his Jacuzzi. Like any proper multimillionaire, Gunther has a full staff of humans to see to his every need. He employs a full-time chauffeur, a gourmet cook, and a personal groomer to keep his hair combed and his teeth brushed. A sports enthusiast, Gunther is the financial backer of the Livorno, Italy, water polo team; and reports received early in 1994 indicated that he was getting ready to buy his own soccer team.

By now you are no doubt wondering how a one-year-old German shepherd could possibly be this wealthy. You know that Gunther could not have acquired such enormous loot from starring in a television series or motion picture, for he's far too young to have collected royalties from any residuals. Besides, the combined salaries of Lassie, Benji and Beethoven would merely add up to a drop in a bucket compared to $80 million dollars. The answer is that, like so many millionaires, Gunther inherited his great wealth from his father, Gunther III.

It seems that back in 1986, the eccentric Austrian countess Carlotta Liebenstein was visiting the Italian village of Fauglia when she spotted Gunther III and developed an immediate fixation upon him. And when she heard him "singing" in his deep-throated howl, her fixation graduated to a full-blown obsession. She even bought a house in the village so that she might be near the handsome German shepherd.

Before the countess's death, she was often heard to express her great disappointment that all people did not love dogs with the same passion that she expressed toward Gunther III. She rewrote her will so that her vast estate would be left to the Gunther Foundation Trust, an organization whose sole task would be to help educate human beings to gain a full understanding of the vast reaches of canine love.

When Countess Liebenstein passed away in 1991, her entire fortune was bequeathed to her beloved shepherd. When Gunther III died a month later, the trust went to his heir, Gunther IV, thus making him the world's richest pet.

At $400 a Month, Booger Boy Can Hope for a Long Life

Certainly not in Gunther IV's league, but comfortable nonetheless, Booger Boy, a six-year-old chow from Chatsworth, Georgia, won the right in a jury trial to receive $400 a month for life from the estate of his deceased owner Martha Jane Dickie.

Martha Jane's will stipulates that her estate will not be divided among her eight human heirs until after Booger Boy's death. And her last testament makes it very clear that any beneficiary found to have been involved in the dog's demise will be summarily disinherited.

His Pets Always Dressed Formally for Dinner

It is not only wealthy or eccentric folks in modern times who have indulged their pets with opulence. In the late eighteenth century, Francis Hendry Egerton, Viscount Brackley, Baron Ellsmere, eighth earl of Bridgewater, ordered his dogs and cats dressed in formal dinner attire and allowed them to dine with him at his table each evening.

A permanent resident of the Hôtel de Noailles in Paris, France, his wealth was extraordinary for his era, his annual income averaging (in today's standards) about $8,000,000. Since Egerton was also a prince of the Holy Roman Empire, his whims and wishes were tolerated by the hotel staff.

The local police, however, grew annoyed with having to deal with his eccentricities, and they continued to be astonished by the man whose house was always full of dogs and cats dressed in elegant finery in the height of fashion. According to contemporary reports, the baron's pets were waited on paw and foot by liveried lackeys. He also maintained a fleet of luxurious coaches at the ready to drive his cats and dogs around the most fashionable sections of the City of Lights.

According to the Wealthy Widow's Will, Cat Father Must Each Year Escort Fifty-two Felines to Mecca

In 1813, a rich Moslem widow in Alexandria, Egypt, left a large fortune to a charitable organization with the provision that the income derived from the sum be devoted completely for the spiritual upliftment of cats.

Each year, according to one of the most extravagant wills in history, fifty-two cats were to be selected to be taken on a pilgrimage to the Holy City of Mecca. The cats, which, of course, had to be considered Moslems, were carefully placed in baskets and loaded on a thoroughbred camel. In charge of their welfare during the pilgrimage was a venerable old man known as the "Cat Father."

All cats who survived the sacred journey were endowed with the honorable title of "hadji," that is, the "perfect pilgrim."

The Heiress and Her Cat Remembered Each Other in Their Wills

Marguerite Mattignon, a seventeenth-century heiress of Paris, France, so loved her favorite cat that she turned over a large share of her fortune to him to be inherited upon her death.

Then, believing reciprocity to be in order, she ordered her attorneys to draw up a will for her cat in which she would be the feline's heir in the event that his nine lives ran out before her own.

Her cat apparently had no problem with such an arrangement, for he signed the document with an inked paw.

Part Five

THE RESCUERS AND THE WARRIORS

Star Dust Comes to the Rescue

Sometimes it almost seems as if a pet is empowered by some higher intelligence to perform acts of bravery and heroism. Ordinary tabbies and undistinguished mutts have suddenly risen to the occasion in most remarkable ways and drawn upon some inner resource to save their human owners from harm.

Can it be, as some religious scholars have speculated, that a person's guardian angel might be able to influence a pet to perform heroic deeds in desperate crisis situations? Or is it simply that our beloved pets may already envision themselves in the role of our "guardian angels"?

Clarisa Bernhardt of Winnipeg, Manitoba, recalled an incident from her own childhood in which it seemed that their much loved black Labrador retriever performed the function of a bona fide guardian angel.

"My sister Katina was about two and one half at the time," she said. "I was several years older. We were outside with the neighbor children playing hopscotch on the driveway between our home and the neighbors'. Our wonderful black lab Star Dust was there with us. She was a shiny, midnight black with a white five-pointed star on her chest, thus her name."

Clarisa remembered that everyone who saw Star Dust always commented on the perfectly shaped and beautiful five-pointed star that she bore. "Her personality was outstanding and she was very friendly, but her unusual star marking just seemed to accentuate her appearance and her countenance. As far as all the neighbor kids were concerned, Star Dust was one of the gang. And we always felt that she understood every word that was said to her."

While the children were growing ever more absorbed in their game of hopscotch, no one noticed that little Katina was stepping off the curb and beginning to stray into the street, which was starting to become very busy with the late afternoon traffic of people returning to their homes from work.

"Mother was just coming out the door to call me to the telephone when she spotted Katina stepping out into the heavy traffic flow," Clarisa said. "Mother screamed as a car came around the corner, moving at a very high rate of speed. It seemed certain that the driver would never be able to see little Katina in time to avoid striking her.

"At the sound of mother's scream, Star Dust became a black streak as she moved with lightning speed toward Katina. She never slowed her pace until she had made contact with Katina. Star Dust opened her jaws and clamped her teeth on the seat of my sister's blue corduroy jumper suit—then she immediately began to back up, pulling Katina out of the path of the oncoming car. The fast-moving automobile missed my little sister by a hair's width!

"The driver stopped the car, but had Star Dust not pulled Katina from its path, it would surely have struck her. The driver told us that as soon as he had seen my sister, he had tried to slow his car and stop, but they never would have been able to avoid hitting her if it had not been for the black Labrador. He couldn't believe his eyes when he saw the manner in which Star Dust had rescued Katina.

"You can imagine the hugs that Star Dust received from all the family, Katina, and the neighborhood kids.

"I want to emphasize that no one had given Star Dust any kind of command that would have sent her out in the street to rescue Katina," Clarisa said. "She made this effort completely on her own. I never saw her move with that speed again. But then, I guess she never needed to. In our family's opinion, she was a very intelligent dog."

As a footnote, Clarisa added that Star Dust was a vegetarian. "She refused to eat meat. She lived to be about fourteen years old before she passed away.

"Interestingly, she appeared to me in a dream just a couple of years ago. She sat down and extended her forepaw. She always liked to 'shake hands.' She seemed happy, and her short message was telepathic and of love."

Pet Cat Awakens Family and Saves Them from Lethal Fumes

In his book *Psychic Pets,* Dennis Bardens tells of an entire family that was rescued due to the selfless ministrations of their pet cat.

One evening in April 1973, Michael Lousada and his two children were asleep in their home in Woburn Sands, England, when fumes that would certainly have proved to be lethal began to leak from a gas-fueled heating boiler. Somehow, to their everlasting gratitude, their cat became alerted to the silent, deadly danger that was moving inexorably throughout their home.

The cat began to mew and scratch noisily and persistently until each of the family members had been awakened and personally made aware of the fatal fumes that had permeated the air in their home.

Weakened by the gas and very near to falling into a coma, Lousada was just barely able to get his children out of the house and to safety. All members of the family recovered from the effects of the gas after a brief stay in the local hospital. They had been saved from greater harm, and even death, by the prompt action of their cat.

Good Neighbor Sam, the Pomeranian

It's pretty difficult for anything to slow down a man as active and helpful to the community as the spry seventy-two-years-young Ken Bakehouse. One night a huge fire broke out that not even Ken could have escaped had it not been for the rescue by his good neighbor Sam.

A professional photographer for forty-five years, Bakehouse has operated a photography studio out of a building which, since 1961, has been joined to his house in Washington, Iowa. He recently was able to pay off entirely the full mortgage on the building and his house so that both were free and clear of debt—but *not* insured.

Comfortably in a deep sleep in his bed, Bakehouse had no idea his buildings were on fire and he was soon to be engulfed in flames.

Meanwhile, next door, Bakehouse's neighbor, Bessie Bell, was trying to figure out why her Pomeranian dog Sam had awakened her with the forbidden act of jumping on her bed. Looking around, Bessie Bell suddenly saw flames shooting out of Bakehouse's building. Bessie frantically dialed 911, but fearing how close the blaze was to her own house, she didn't wait to talk with the 911 dispatcher.

"Let's get out of here; we're not going to burn," Bessie said to Sam. Now fearing she might fall while trying to escape, Bessie managed to push her emergency "life line" button which also summoned help.

Fortunately, even without having provided a dispatcher with the particulars about the 911 call, thanks to technology, the call had registered the location of the incoming call at the sheriff's department. It didn't take long for a police car and ambulance to arrive, with the fire department not far behind.

At 1:15 A.M., a startled Ken Bakehouse awakened to hear a shout, "Hey, your building is on fire!" Although Bakehouse made it to safety, just about everything burned. He lost his entire studio and all his equipment. Because of the exorbitant premiums to insure the photography equipment and developing chemicals, Ken was without insurance. The damage incurred was a minimum of $50,000.

It's been hard going for Bakehouse. Within a short period of time, his wife suffered a stroke which left her in need of full-time assistance in a care center; and his daughter was just recently diagnosed with cancer—then, this horrible fire.

It would be easy for the best of us to feel down and in despair with so much to bear at one time. But it was clear to us that God must have a plan for sparing Bakehouse through the alert actions of good neighbor Sam, the Pomeranian. Bakehouse responded to our sympathy by saying: "I'm so grateful that, even though I've lost everything—I have my life! I'm not going to let the devil steal my joy!

"I could have been seriously burned—or worse—died," Ken continued, "but the things that burned were only material." This sentiment would have been fresh on his mind, for an amazing irony to Bakehouse's story is that only several days earlier he had seen how the ravages of fire had forever changed the life of a wonderful lady.

Bakehouse had helped Christie Humphries set up for a concert after a long absence. Christie had been a very successful and accomplished pianist whose life and career had been horribly interrupted by a brutal fire that left her very seriously injured.

This return engagement was heartrending, considering the very long, difficult and painful period of strenuous rehabilitation required for Christie to play again—especially considering that the fire left Christie with burns on over 85 percent of her body. She was left with only five fingers with which to play the piano—five fingers—between *both* hands!

Realizing that he could have been in that condition himself had it not been for the wonderful little dog next door, Bakehouse said to us: "Man, with what Christie went through, what have I got to complain about!"

Ken keeps a positive attitude. Even though his career was wiped out by the loss of all his equipment and studio, he's been keeping himself busy by writing songs.

Uncertain if he will be able to get his photography business back together at this point, Ken has been working with less expensive equipment—paper and pencil! In spite of his trials he has managed to write words and music to more than seventy inspirational songs he's hoping might be uplifting to others—who might also be going through tough times.

It Was Payback Time for Sheena

Thirty-nine-year-old John Rayner of St. Petersburg, Florida, had his back broken twice and must walk with a cane. Perhaps his own physical condition helped him to feel great empathy when a few years ago he found a female shepherd mix badly injured in his yard.

It was apparent to John that she had been struck by a car and had managed to crawl to safety on his property. Since she had no license or identification tags, it was also apparent that the injured dog was a stray.

John patiently and lovingly nursed the dog, whom he named Sheena, back to health, and the two became inseparable pals.

Recently, when John was heading back to his car after stopping at a market for a few groceries, two punks approached him and demanded his wallet and his watch. Sheena, who was inside the car, began to bark fiercely.

Forced to walk with a cane because of his crippling accidents, John managed to use the walking stick as a weapon, and he knocked one of the thugs out cold.

But his act of defiance sent the other hoodlum into a rage, and he began to hit John with violent, powerful blows. As his assailant spun him around against the car, John thought that a knife in his ribs would probably be his fate.

Somehow, though, John managed to reach out and open the car door. Sheena hurled herself from within and struck the hoodlum full in the chest, knocking him to the ground.

John could clearly see the terror in his attacker's eyes as Sheena's bared teeth snapped scant inches from his face.

The thug managed to push Sheena off him, and he took off running, the dog barking and snapping at his heels.

As John limped toward the store to call for help, the punk that he had knocked cold regained consciousness, looked around at a very different scene—one in which he and his partner were the victims—and he, too, ran off.

When John returned from making his call to the police, Sheena was heading back to the car with a definite air of triumph exuding from her confident trot. As he hugged her to his chest, John thanked her for returning the favor. She had now saved his life as he had saved hers.

They Saved Their Master from a Watery Grave in an Icy Lake

Chris Georgiou runs a trout-fishing farm outside of Adelaide, Australia, a picturesque place where people can toss their fishing lines in a dammed area of a lake. On this particular winter's day in 1992, no would-be fisher folk had arrived, so Chris was making use of the off-day to catch up on some maintenance chores.

Actually, he was completely alone on the farm—with the exception of his two dogs—for his wife was far away in Africa on vacation.

As Chris chopped at the tall grass growing near the dam, his two-year-old Border collie Ziggy was at his side, and Stella, his two-year-old rottweiler, was dozing outside of the house about sixty yards away.

Chris rose to straighten himself from the bending posture that he was forced to assume as he chopped at the tall grass on the bank, and he accidentally struck his head a solid rap on the iron railing that surrounds the fishing area.

Stunned, he lost his balance and toppled into the icy water. Because it was a chilly day, Chris was wearing a heavy wool sweater, a thick coat, overalls and boots, and the bulky clothing caused him to sink as if he were bound with iron weights. Such heavy clothing would have challenged even an accomplished swimmer, but the sixty-six-year-old trout farmer had never learned to swim a stroke.

Flailing his arms desperately and shouting for help, Chris knew it was only a matter of moments before he went down for good. The more he struggled to stay afloat, the farther from shore he propelled himself.

Ziggy stood on the bank, sounding a shrill, frightened bark. It was so obvious that he wanted to help his master, but he seemed to know that his little twenty-five-pound body could not keep both of them afloat.

Coughing, sputtering, realizing that his struggle was nearly over,

Chris thought the last sound that he would hear on earth was the shrill, mournful bark of his faithful Ziggy.

"Then a miracle happened," Chris Georgiou told journalist Chris Pritchard. "There, leaping out from the bank in midair, was my rottweiler Stella. Her body hurtled out across the water like a rocket, then plopped down into the water alongside me."

Chris managed to get hold of Stella's right leg, and the powerfully built ninety-pound rottweiler began towing him slowly toward the bank.

The miracle held long enough for an exhausted Chris Georgiou to emerge from the shallows, drag himself up the wooden steps leading out of the dam, and to collapse out of harm's way. Then the two dogs were joyously licking at his face.

It now became clear to Chris that little Ziggy had desperately wanted to jump into the lake to save him, but he had the wisdom to understand that he was too small to rescue a big man weighted down by heavy clothing. That was why he had barked so shrilly and alerted the snoozing Stella, who was strong as a bull, to come quickly and save their master's life.

Chris freely admitted that he hugged his two dogs and "cried like a baby." They had certainly proved that they were his best friends.

Born Without a Bark, Sable Had to Lick His Master to Safety

According to the fire chiefs in Dallas, Texas, in another ten minutes Stephen Helliar's entire house would have gone up in flames, and there would have been no hope of saving anyone's life.

If Sable had been born with a bark, her rescue of her master and his housemate would have been a lot easier.

As it was, on that fateful night early in 1991, she had to run upstairs through thick, billowing black smoke and leap onto Stephen's bed and keep giving him big, slobbery kisses until he woke up.

When the wet, doggy kisses finally accomplished their goal, Stephen, twenty-five, saw that the bedroom was filled with smoke. Jarred into wakefulness, he rushed downstairs, where he could see that the kitchen stove was engulfed in flames.

With the faithful Sable at his side, Stephen found that his housemate, Jane Lindsay, had already been overcome by smoke and was unconscious. They dragged her to safety, and Stephen spent four minutes working to revive her before help arrived.

Stephen and Jane freely acknowledge that, without Sable's slobbery kisses, they both would have perished in the fire.

As for Sable, she fortunately suffered only a few singed areas on her short-haired coat and a slightly burned front paw.

It Certainly Paid to Give These Two Stray Dogs a Home

A while back, Susan Terrell was waiting in the parking lot of a store for her husband Allen to finish shopping when she saw the driver of a passing pickup truck throw a newborn puppy out of the window.

The poor little thing was skinned up from being tossed out of the window of a moving vehicle, but seemed otherwise all right. The Terrells took him home and named him Misty.

Not too long after that, they opened their front door one night to find a dirty, starved, homeless dog covered with ticks standing there, begging to be let in. They adopted him, too, and named him Max.

What ye sow, so shall ye reap, applies to caring for our four-legged little brothers and sisters, as well. Early in 1994, the Terrells of Lubbock, Texas, were awakened in the middle of the night by Misty and Max barking up a storm. Once startled out of their sleep, Allen and Susan soon determined that their house was on fire.

The Terrells were able to escape from harm and to summon firefighters before the flames got out of hand and completely destroyed their home. Damage was estimated at around $10,000, but experts affirmed that it could have been much worse if the dogs hadn't alerted them to the fire.

Yes, the damage could have been worse. But that wouldn't have mattered much if Max and Misty had not first saved the lives of the two kind animal lovers who had taken them in and given them a home.

Dog Cushions Boy's Fall in an Amazing Catch

Eleven-year-old Alfredo Iannone of Salerno, Italy, no doubt knew very well in the back of his mind that he and his friend should not be climbing around on the roof of a building under construction. That thought probably acquired a whole new dimension of truth when he walked too near the edge and tripped.

As he plummeted through space, Alfredo remembered screaming and thinking that he would surely die.

If not death, then surely terrible injury would have been his fate from having fallen thirty-five feet if it had not been for Stella, his big, part-German shepherd, who made a selfless dash to position herself directly under her master's falling body.

Later, Alfredo recalled that it had been "like falling onto a mattress." In front of startled eyewitnesses, the boy bounced off the back of the stalwart Stella and onto the ground. Except for a few bruises, he was completely unharmed. Stella, too, was none the worse for wear for having served as living safety net for her careless master.

Alfredo's friend said that Stella had been barking at them from below, as if she were warning them to be careful and scolding them for being so foolhardy. Stella had "run like a bullet" to position herself under Alfredo.

A physician at the Salerno Public Hospital was yet another voice of praise who declared Stella a hero. In his opinion, Alfredo would have been killed if the big dog had not raced under him to cushion his fall.

Burt Is Transformed from Parrot to Bodyguard When His Mistress Is Threatened

Tawnya Sutherland of Kearns, Utah, had just returned home after visiting a friend on the afternoon of February 6, 1994, when she found herself in the middle of every young girl's worst nightmare. She was home alone, and there was a burly stranger in their kitchen.

The blonde seventeen-year-old high school junior screamed at the man to get out of their house, but the big man just glared at her. At five-feet-six, 125 pounds, she knew that she was no match for a six-footer who weighed well over 200 pounds.

As the brute began to move toward her, Tawnya could hear Burt, her Amazon parrot, whistling for her, just as he always did when he heard her come home. Burt, her feathered buddy for five years, was fiercely protective of her, but she expected little help from the one-pound bird against an intruder the size of the creep who threatened her now.

In desperation, Tawnya threw a glass at the man, but he easily sidestepped the missile.

As he closed in on her, she kicked him in the groin, but he only grunted and seemed annoyed, rather than injured.

The monster grabbed her shirt and hit her hard in the ribs.

Tawnya told reporter Susan Fenton that at this point in the desperate drama, she felt "something too horrible to imagine was about to happen to me."

But that was when little one-pound Burt became amazingly transformed into a tough and relentless bodyguard.

Squawking a terrible battle cry, Burt flew into the kitchen, landed on the thug's shoulder, and began biting his neck.

Tawnya feared for her brave little bird, because it seemed as though the attacker would be able to demolish him with one solid blow of his heavy hands. But Burt had launched a kamikaze attack, and it was obvious that nothing would make him let go of the brute who threatened his mistress. And no matter how the intruder twisted and turned, the enraged parrot could not be shaken loose of his clawhold on his shoulder. And those claws and beak were drawing blood!

The teenager was stunned when she beheld yet another remarkable transformation. The big, brutish thug was changing into a "sniveling crybaby" right before her eyes.

When the stranger at last managed to break away from the pain inflicted by Burt's beak and claws, he ran out the back door, cursing his agony as he ran.

The courageous Burt flew to Tawnya to see if she was all right. The grateful teenager could see that her brave bird was exhausted from the awful struggle, and she began to work at quieting him and reassuring him that he had saved the day and everything was now okay.

Later, Deputy Jim Potter, of the Salt Lake County sheriff's office, said that in his twenty years of police work this was the first incident that he had encountered in which a bird went to the aid of its owner.

Tawnya's mother admitted that she had often teased her daughter about the protectiveness of her parrot. She said that she would not do so anymore. Brave Burt saved Tawnya from great possible injury.

Courageous Cat Saves Two-Year-Old from Bear

Pet lovers have often observed the strange phenomenon of a small dog or cat that simply does not seem to perceive how tiny it really is in comparison to an attacker. We once observed a bitsy Chihuahua make a Great Dane back down when the little gal felt that the big brute was threatening her mistress. On another occasion, we were about to run to the aid of a small cat being circled by three stray dogs, but by the time we had arrived, the diminutive feline had sent them all packing with her own brand of kitty kung fu.

And, it would appear, as with humans, such an indefinable element as courage seems to remain an individual matter that is next to impossible to predict. Monster mastiffs bred to defend their masters at all costs turn into whimpering cowards at the slightest threat, while seemingly passive pussy cats summon the law of the jungle and transform themselves into the King of Beasts when danger approaches.

During their summer vacation in 1993, John and Cassandra Kraven headed for a cottage in the Adirondack Mountains in upstate New York with their two-year-old daughter Jane—and their cat, Socks, named after the president's feline. Actually, they had not wanted to bring the cat along, fearing that it would be too much bother, but a friend who was supposed to kitty-sit was called out of town at the last minute.

The first few days at the cottage had truly been relaxing, but their tranquility was nearly irreparably shattered when a black bear suddenly stormed into their yard. Before John or Cassandra could respond to the situation from within the freeze frame of shock that had enveloped them, the huge animal had grabbed their daughter and was shaking her in his snout as if she were a rag doll.

At that moment of ultimate horror, Socks leaped onto the bear's head, fastened his back claws into its flesh, and scratched at the brute's eyes until it dropped the baby in order to better direct its wrath at the attack cat.

Socks, beholding victory with Jane now released from the behemoth's jaws, jumped to the ground and deftly avoided the clumsy giant's swiping paws. Then, with the bear in hot pursuit, Socks ran into the forest.

John and Cassandra ran to their child, who, though crying in terror, seemed unharmed. Miraculously, the bear's teeth had snatched at the girl's playsuit and had not punctured her flesh. If it hadn't been for Socks' dramatic intervention, however, they were horrified to think of what might have happened.

After about two hours, Socks returned to the cabin, completely unharmed. The Kravens theorize that their courageous kitty led the bear on a merry chase deep into the forest, far away from their cabin, in order to insure the return of peace and quiet for the remainder of their vacation.

John and Cassandra know that they owe their daughter's life to

Socks, the cat that they wanted to leave behind. They said that they will never visit their cottage again unless they are in the company of their fierce attack cat.

The Dogs of Project Safe Run Are Always Ready to Take a Bite Out of Muggers!

When she was twenty years old, Shelley Reecher of Eugene, Oregon, was brutally abducted and assaulted in broad daylight while she was jogging.

Understandably, after surviving such a terrible experience, she became frightened by the very prospect of jogging alone. She tried to coordinate her running schedule with that of fellow joggers, but that became increasingly difficult to manage.

That was when she thought of training a dog to be her jogging buddy. She would set about converting man's best friend into a mugger's worst nightmare.

She went to a pound, selected a sturdy Doberman pinscher, named him Jake, and trained him to run with her. With Jake at her side, she felt safe.

It wasn't long before other women were asking Shelley if they might borrow Jake on their runs, but that became increasingly difficult to arrange with her own schedule.

The solution seemed obvious: She would just have to train more dogs to keep up with the demand for hazard-free jogging for women.

Today, approximately eighteen years later, Shelley Reecher's non-profit program, Project Safe Run, will provide a woman with a canine jogging companion for a modest monthly fee. German shepherds, rottweilers and Dobermans are available to run with the ladies twenty-four hours a day, seven days a week. Project Safe Run currently has chapters in Chicago, New York City, Los Angeles, Gainesville, Florida, as well as Eugene, Oregon, and a number of cities in the Pacific Northwest.

Ms. Reecher stresses that each of the canine bodyguards enters a rugged eight-week defensive training program and is taught never to provoke or to initiate an attack. Their sole mission is to protect the lady runner from being assaulted.

Project Safe Run dogs are programmed first to growl and bark in an attempt to frighten away a mugger. The dogs will attack a persistent aggressor only as a last resort.

Once a dog has passed the course and has been running on the job, it is regularly monitored to keep it healthy. Its brain is kept sharp by a series of refresher courses and occasional simulated attacks to keep them always on the ready.

Thus far, in well over 9,000 runs, Project Safe Run maintains a perfect record. There has not been one attack attempted on a jogger. Nor has there been a single accidental biting of any innocent party.

Look Who's Guarding the Sheep: Donkeys!

Texas sheepherders and goat ranchers raise nearly four million sheep and Angora goats annually, but recent federal environmental restrictions on traps and poisons have created a big problem with marauding coyotes.

"As the coyote population grew in ever-larger numbers, our herd losses moved up the scale with them," a Texas sheepherder said. "We began to lose upward of nine million dollars in livestock each year."

The classic sheep dogs that one sees in motion pictures cost a lot of money to purchase and a great deal of time to train. And once a trained dog is performing efficiently, it quite naturally has to be fed regularly or the sheep are going to start looking very tasty to its hungry eyes.

The answer to the ranchers' problem finally revealed itself in the humble figure of the braying donkey.

Once a donkey has established its territory, it becomes extremely possessive of its turf. Donkeys have a natural disliking for coyotes, wolves and dogs, and they will immediately attack any prowling coyote with hooves and teeth, driving the predator away or even killing it.

As one rancher put it, "All you have to do is to drop a donkey off near your herd and forget about it. It will make friends with the sheep or goats, establish its territory, and protect the critters against predators around the clock. And you don't need to bring food out to the donkey two or three times a day. It will forage for itself on the grasses growing in the area. Besides, donkeys are vegetarians and don't eat meat."

Another rancher emphasized the often-ignored fact that donkeys are highly intelligent. "Folklore and fables have made the poor donkey the butt of so many jokes that make the animal out to be stupid. It just isn't so. And the donkey also has a great level of endurance and hardly ever gets sick."

An official with the Texas Agriculture Department stated that the donkey has filled an important need in helping ranchers protect their stock. According to recent estimates, more than 1,800 Texas sheep and goat ranchers have now turned to guard donkeys, which can cost as little as $150 each.

When sheep herders in Alberta, Canada, began to complain of increased losses due to coyote attacks on their flocks, the province's department of agriculture suggested that they begin to use guard donkeys as their protectors.

Although highly skeptical at first, a rancher near Vermillion, in Alberta, who had been bedeviled by coyotes raiding his livestock pens, said that he had no problems after his guard donkey arrived.

Another rancher who complained that he had lost twenty-six goats and six lambs in two months to the wily coyotes admitted that he had hired a guard donkey only as a last resort. "We had been terrorized by packs of coyotes for eight years," he said. "But from the day that we got our guard donkey, we have not lost a single animal to predators."

One rancher commented about the friendship that develops between a guard donkey and his fleecy buddies. "The sheep seem to accept the donkey as a member of the flock."

Beware of the Lady's Watch Hog

When attractive, twenty-six-year-old Roslyn Stewart is out walking Bud and Alfie, muggers, mashers and molesters had better give them a wide berth. Alfie, is a German shepherd, and Bud is a Vietnamese pot-bellied porker that devoutly believes that he is a vicious watch hog.

"The dog barks and the pig bites," their owner Ms. Stewart is quick to announce.

It immediately becomes very clear that, together, the two make a perfect pair of four-legged bodyguards.

The house-trained porker could easily tip the scales at 150 pounds when he achieves his full dimensions. Ms. Stewart acquired the pig just a few months before she got the German shepherd, and she raised the two together as pals.

Dog and hog patrol Roslyn's home near Amersham, England, and keep wary eyes and keen nostrils on the alert for intruders. Her boyfriend, American stuntman Bobby Ore, feels much more at ease when he is away, just knowing that Bud and Alfie are standing sentry duty.

Roslyn admitted that Bud had bitten a delivery man and a gamekeeper and had chased away dozens of uninvited salesmen. She advised that if the pig takes a liking to a stranger, he will wag his skinny little tail, just like Alfie. Should he not be favorably impressed with a stranger, she warned, Bud lowers his head and charges.

"He truly is a force to be reckoned with," she acknowledged.

Dog They Wanted to Put to Sleep Saved Owner's Life

Lord knows, it wasn't because they didn't love Trixie that they decided she should be put to sleep. It was just that the poor little dachshund had an incurable skin disease that the veterinarian called allergic dermatitis, which caused an endless itching and a discoloration of the skin.

The medical bills were becoming a terrible drain upon the limited resources of Roberta and Claude Peterson of Baton Rouge, Louisiana, usually totaling about seventy-five dollars a month. And then there were the special food preparations that Trixie had to eat. They, too, were expensive.

And since Claude, seventy-eight, had diabetes, and they both had heart problems, they no longer had the physical energy that taking proper care of Trixie required.

But when the seventy-one-year-old Roberta took Trixie to the veterinarian, Dr. Al Haase talked her out of putting the eight-year-old dachshund to sleep.

Feeling somewhat guilty that they had even entertained such a thought, Roberta agreed with the vet that Trixie shouldn't be eliminated because of circumstances which were no fault of her own.

It was only a few months later when Trixie repaid her debt of continued life in full. Claude suffered a severe insulin reaction and fainted in the bathroom. As he fell into the bathtub, he cut his arm deeply enough so that he could have bled to death if left unattended for very long.

Trixie, however, was on the alert. She ran into the room where Roberta was watching television, jumped up on her lap, barked at her, then jumped off and began tugging at her bathrobe, pulling her toward the bathroom. Opening the door, Roberta was stunned to discover her husband slumped over the tub, bleeding profusely from his arm.

By the time Claude reached the hospital, he was in a coma. It took five hours for the medical staff to get his blood sugar level back to normal so that they could feel right about releasing him.

Roberta and Claude said that they owed Trixie their heartfelt thanks for the opportunity of celebrating their fifty-second wedding anniversary.

Dr. Haase nominated Trixie for the Louisiana Veterinary Medical Association's 1992 "Pet of the Year" award, and the committee agreed with his recommendation.

The Baton Rouge veterinarian told writer Chanda Peterkin that Trixie was a real hero, deserving of the award. "People can learn from her story that animals are special and courageous creatures."

Foxy Rang the Bell and Brought Help for His Elderly Owner

On December 8, 1966, a small fox terrier was responsible for bringing aid to its injured mistress, Mrs. W.Z. Robinette, eighty-four, of Gate City, Virginia.

Mrs. Robinette had fallen on the concrete walkway in front of her home and had broken her hip. Unable to move, the elderly woman lay helpless in her pain. Her feeble cries for help failed to elicit any type of response from her nearby neighbors.

Then Foxy, her terrier, bounded into view.

Cocking his head quizzically from side to side, Foxy seemed to be thinking the situation over very carefully.

"I . . . need . . . help," Mrs. Robinette managed to force past her pain.

Foxy whined his sympathy in apparent understanding, and he began to pace nervously around the form of his fallen mistress.

Suddenly, his attention seemed to be directed to an outside dinner bell.

Mrs. Robinette followed Foxy's intent gaze and groaned aloud—this time in despair and frustration, rather than pain.

Because Foxy had been taking canine delight in occasionally grabbing the rope and ringing the bell, she had only recently tied the rope up out of the terrier's reach so that he might not annoy the neighbors.

The new height of the rope seemed not to bother Foxy's planning. Although he had not rung the bell since his mistress had scolded him and proceeded to tie the rope up out of his reach, he seemed to understand that in the light of the present emergency, all would be forgiven if he were to accomplish an Olympic-like leap and make the bell ring for all it was worth.

Summoning hidden resources of energy, Foxy leaped three feet into the air, snatched the rope in his teeth, and brought forth a resounding ringing of the bell. Again and again, the little fox terrier jumped high and yanked the rope with his teeth.

Foxy seemed justifiably pleased with himself when Mrs. Robinette's nearest neighbor came running to his mistress' side.

The concerned neighbor immediately summoned an ambulance, and Mrs. Robinette was on her way to a hospital for treatment. While she recovered under medical care, Foxy was cared for in a manner that befitted a hero.

Minni, the World's Bravest Poodle

Although to the undiscerning eye she might appear to be nothing more than a pint-sized poodle, Minni seems to have made a kind of career out of using her wits and saving human lives.

Silvana Morani, Minni's owner, is justifiably proud of the petite black poodle who has twice saved her life, rescued a little girl from drowning in the ocean, and alerted an entire village to an armed attack.

According to Ms. Morani, a high school biology teacher in Milan, Italy, Minni first proved her selfless courage in 1975 when she accompanied her mistress on a research trip to a village in Senegal, Africa.

Rebels from neighboring Guinea-Bissau (formerly Portuguese Guinea) were hiding in the village; and unbeknownst to the villagers, soldiers who were pursuing the rebels were about to attack. But then, Ms. Morani said, Minni detected the movement in the brush of the encircling men and began barking furiously, thus alerting villagers to the threat and miraculously frightening the soldiers away.

On one occasion, Ms. Morani suffered a freak accident that could have cost her life if Minni had not been vigilant.

"I had been taking a hot bath, and the high temperature suddenly caused my circulatory system to collapse," Ms. Morani said. She found herself unable to move, everything began to turn black, and she started to lose consciousness.

Minni, however, sensed her mistress' problem, began a loud barking, and summoned Ms. Morani's mother, who immediately called a doctor.

Silvana Morani confesses her prejudice, but insists that her Minni is the "most courageous animal in the world." By winter of 1991, the long-lived poodle had received such worldwide honors as the following:

- Honored by Pope John Paul II at the Vatican in recognition of God's love for animals.
- Awarded the Italian national prize for dog fidelity, given to animals who show extraordinary courage and love to humans.
- Named "Queen of the Animals" during an international award ceremony in India and presented with gold equal to her weight. Ms. Morani donated the prize to charities for animals.

Beaky the Dolphin to the Rescue

In the early 1970s, Bob Holborn, a plumber turned deep sea diver, trained a Cornish dolphin to become an accomplished lifeguard. "Beaky" was responsible for the saving of many lives in the waters off Land's End.

Author Dennis Bardens quotes Holborn telling of the time when a foreign sailor fell off the side of a boat and Beaky held him up in the water for several hours until help finally arrived.

On another occasion, it was one of Holborn's own friends who was diving off Land's End when a sudden thick fog separated him from his boat. "Beaky actually took him to the steps of his diving boat and saved his life."

According to Holborn, on April 20, 1976, an accomplished diver named Keith Monery found himself in a desperate situation off Penzance, Cornwall. He could no longer rely on his life jacket, for it had become filled with water. Well experienced in the water, Monery had already discarded his fifteen-pound weight belt, but he was still having great difficulty reaching the surface.

The sea had become rough, and he was rapidly nearing exhaustion. Although a friend saw Monery's distress signal—a clenched fist waved frantically to and fro—and dove in the water to attempt a rescue, Bardens writes that another "friend" was quicker:

"Beaky streaked past [the human rescuer] like a rocket. The friendly mammal . . . got underneath its human friend and kept pushing him, again and again, to the surface, until he was rescued."

Her "Dumb" Dog Saved Her from a House Fire

Betty Kitson of Concord, New Hampshire, had never really thought that Moses, her two-year-old Labrador-golden retriever mix, was really all that bright. Although no one could question the blind woman's affection for her dog, she made no secret of her opinion that Moses was of rather short supply in the brains department.

Then on Wednesday morning, January 19, 1994, a fire broke out, and wonder of wonders, the dumb dog courageously led his blind owner to safety.

Betty told the Associated Press that she couldn't even begin "to fathom" what Moses had done for her. She knew that he was able to "sit pretty for a bone," but until that fateful day, she thought that was about as far as his talents went.

When the fire broke out, she dropped to all-fours, grabbed Moses' collar, then just followed the big dog to safety.

"He led me out of that room. He really did," Betty Kitson declared in pride and amazement.

Noble Neighbors Shelter Pooch from Death Sentence

On occasion, of course, it behooves humans to come to the rescue of a pet. Quite different from dragging a pet from a burning building or protecting it from violent attackers, the men and women to whom we pay tribute in this segment banded together in a conspiracy to rescue an innocent dog from a cruel and thoughtless administration of the law.

When eighty-five-year-old Ethel Harris of Minehead, England, died in March 1991, her will gave clear instructions that Benjy, her faithful terrier, should be put to sleep. Mrs. Harris had no pretensions of assuming the pomp of an ancient pharaoh entering the burial chamber with her possessions—both inanimate and animate—laid to rest beside her. She wished Benjy to join her in death only because she feared that he would be neglected after she had made her transition.

But the sweet, lovable Benjy, a ten-year-old Jack Russell terrier, had also won the hearts of Mrs. Harris's neighbors, and they were shocked when they learned that their elderly friend's will had pronounced a death sentence on everyone's favorite dog. Consequently, when the lawyers tried to carry out the dictates of Mrs. Harris's will, they found that Benjy had been dognapped.

Not gentlemen to be thwarted in the fulfillment of their instructions, the barristers summoned the police to search out the doomed terrier.

But the neighbors banded together in precision teamwork and smuggled Benjy from house to house while the police dutifully scoured the area.

One of the neighbors approached the attorneys to plead Benjy's case. He told the counselors that old Mrs. Harris had truly loved the dog, but she had become a bit confused near the end. If she knew that Benjy was well taken care of and provided with a good home, she would be happy. Why, the eloquent neighbor asked the barristers, couldn't everyone just consider the matter settled?

An officious attorney sternly informed the well-intentioned pooch protector that the law was the law—and it must be carried out to its fullest letter. Benjy must be put to death according to the provisions of Mrs. Harris's will.

Faced with such an ultimatum, the neighborhood dognappers saw that they had only two choices: (1) deliver Benjy to be put to death according to the decree pronounced in Mrs. Harris's will, or (2) assist Benjy in becoming a full-fledged fugitive.

In no time at all the neighborhood jury had reached its decision. One of the dognappers put Benjy in his car and drove the condemned terrier hundreds of miles away, where a good, loving home awaited him.

As far as we know, the loyal and noble neighbors have maintained their pact of silence as to the pooch's actual whereabouts, and Benjy continues to live out his life in a town far away from Minehead—where he is still wanted by the law!

Part Six

THE POWER OF LOVE THAT BINDS US WITH OUR PETS IN THE ONENESS OF ALL LIFE

A Dog Named Lola Taught Him the Power of Love

Stan Kalson of Phoenix, Arizona, said that he now understands that the dog Lola's arrival in his life was no coincidence.

"Long ago I realized that there really are no coincidences, only serendipitous happenings which unfold to give us our lessons on our life's journey," he said.

For over a year, Stan recalled, he had been searching for a special dog to replace his Australian shepherd, Andrew, who had "eloped" with a female German shepherd who was visiting the mountain resort that he coowned in Strawberry, Arizona.

Andrew had long been Stan's good buddy, traveling everywhere with him. Strangers meeting Andrew for the first time always commented on his apparent sensitivity, intelligence and loving nature. Time and again, people would express the identical observation: "This dog is almost human!"

And then came that eventful day when Andrew signaled telepathically to Stan that he would prefer to live with his new friend, Shanti, the German shepherd.

"Reluctantly I released him to be happy in his new situation," he said. "Everyone was shocked that I allowed Andrew to leave. They all knew how close we were. My response was that our deep love allowed me to permit Andrew to follow his own path."

After a few months of being "dogless," however, Stan began to peruse the dog section of the daily newspaper, keeping his eye out for any ads offering Australian shepherds. "My logical mind argued that my present life situation would not really permit my owning another dog, but my emotional being kept telling me, 'yes, get another dog.' It seemed as though I were holding constant battles in my subconscious for the perfect Australian shepherd to manifest in my life."

Then one day as he was reading the classified section of the Mogollon *Advisor*, Stan found the answer to his inner yearing: FREE TO GOOD HOME; ONE LOVING AUSTRALIAN SHEPHERD FEMALE.

Stan's heart raced. Could this be his new dog, just one day before his birthday in May?

He immediately called the present owner of the dog and was soon chatting pleasantly with a lady named Sarah, who told him that she had found the dog two and a half years before, "abandoned, skinny, and desperately wanting love." Sarah's family named her Lola and intended to keep her for only a short time. As things had worked out, Lola had produced a litter of puppies, and now her family agreed that she deserved to receive the attention that would be focused on "the only dog in the family."

A few hours later, Sarah arrived at Stan's place with a van load of dogs. Lola jumped out and immediately made friendly contact with him. Such outwardness on the part of Lola surprised Sarah, who commented that the dog was usually cautious with strangers.

"I loved her and connected with her immediately," Stan recalled. "The little boy in me asked, 'Can I keep her?'"

Sarah told him Lola was all his. Stan had been the only person who had responded to the newspaper ad.

Sarah sadly hugged Lola goodbye, then drove back down the hill. "Lola let out the most heartfelt sounds of loss and sorrow," Stan said. "I comforted her until the wailing sounds ceased."

Although he was delighted to have ended his search for an Australian shepherd to take the place of Andrew, Lola's arrival happened to have occurred on an extremely busy day for Stan.

"I had no choice other than to chain her to a tree so I could accomplish my many tasks. Lola barked and barked, and I realized that she needed my attention," Stan said.

A well-intentioned visitor, unaware that Stan had acquired the dog only minutes before, assured him that he should let Lola off the chain. "She won't run away," he said confidently.

Too busy to think it through rationally, Stan followed the visitor's advice.

"Lola immediately ran off into the forest, and I wondered why I had done such a dumb thing," Stan remembered. "I called Sarah and asked her to watch for Lola, then I began sending loving thought-messages to Lola, asking her to come back to me. Two hours later, she sheepishly returned, her actions reflecting that she had 'heard' me telling her that I wanted her and that I loved her. I never had to chain her again."

For the next few days, Lola cautiously observed Stan and shadowed his every movement throughout the day. He constantly reassured her with hugs, walks, gourmet food and lots of love.

"Within a few days, it felt as though Lola and I had been together for many lifetimes," Stan said. "Resort visitors would comment on our close relationship and how well-behaved Lola was. The spring and summer months were filled with many adventures as Lola and I walked in the forest."

When fall came and it was time to return to Phoenix for the winter months, Lola eagerly jumped into the car for the departure to the big city.

Within days of Stan's return to Phoenix, his attorney called about some business matters that needed to be discussed. Since it was apparent that their meeting would take several hours, he decided to take Lola along with him.

Once they arrived at Stan's attorney's home, the man's wife suggested that Lola would be more comfortable with a bone in their walled-in back yard while the two fellows proceeded on to the office.

"Three hours later, I discovered that Lola was gone," Stan recalled. "The evidence of a hole dug at the base of the back yard wall proved that Lola had escaped to find me. I freaked out at the thought of Lola, used to forest trails and country life, wandering alone in a big city. I didn't have any identification on her, and I feared that I might never seen her again."

Siglinde, his attorney's wife, took Stan by the hand, and they began to search the nearby streets, calling Lola's name.

"For two hours we called for Lola, walking up and down streets adjacent to my attorney's home. It seemed apparent that Lola was no longer within earshot of our calls. I considered releasing Lola to the Highest Good for her return to me—or to her finding another loving home."

Stan deeply felt his loss as he drove the fifteen miles to his house. It was nearly 1:00 A.M. when he finally closed his eyes.

"At four o'clock I bolted up from my sleep, and I heard my inner voice tell me to go back to the area where I had lost Lola," Stan said.

"It was still dark, and I intuitively felt that I would wait until daylight to retrace my drive across town."

A while later, half asleep, Stan drove on Thomas Road, which was not customarily his return route to his attorney's house. Since it was still dark, he stopped to read his mail at the post office at 40th Street and Thomas Road.

"I read through my mail until I saw the first signs of daylight," Stan said, "then I proceeded across Thomas Road. As I approached 16th Street, I was startled to see Lola in the middle of the street making a turn north on 16th Street, sniffing the air as she dodged the cars.

"The timing was unbelievable! Just a few moments later, and I would have missed her.

"I made a turn north on 16th Street, honking my horn at Lola, which only made her run faster.

"I stuck my head out the window and bellowed: 'Lola! Lola!'

"She stopped, turned around, and leaped through my open window into my arms, as cries of joy were emitted from both of us."

Stan stopped the car and held Lola in his arms for several moments. As soon as he had collected his thoughts, he telephoned Siglinde, his attorney's wife, who exclaimed that it was a miracle straight from a Higher Source that had reunited him with Lola.

On his way home, Stan stopped at the office of his best friend, Lee Lage, to tell her the great news. A client in Lee's waiting room overheard him tell the story of his finding Lola, and as Stan walked to the door, she stopped him.

"It was the love that you held in your heart for your dog and the love of God for both you and your pet that reunited you," she told him. "You and your dog must be special!"

"As I walked out of the office," Stan remembered, "tears streamed down my face as I felt the great power of God's love!"

We are pleased to include the following fascinating account of a rat's remarkable intelligence and love as it was presented to us by Dr. P.M.H. Atwater, an internationally recognized authority on near-death phenomena and spiritual transformations. Dr. Atwater's Coming Back to Life: The After-Effects of the Near-Death Experience *(Ballantine Books, 1989) has become a classic in its field. For information about her research into the near-death experience and special audio tapes produced by Dr. Atwater, write to her in care of Ellen Lively Steele, PO Box 468, Organ, NM 88052.*

The Mysterious Return of DeeDee, the Educated Rat

It was the last day of school before summer vacation. The sixth grade teacher busily assisted each student in cleaning out desks, lockers and storage areas. Volunteers were requested, so all classroom pets could be adopted. My youngest daughter Paulie happily raised her hand.

That's how it happened. Without my permission or knowledge or any form of advance preparation, a most unusual rat named DeeDee accompanied my daughter home from school. She came to live with us.

DeeDee was a hooded rat (white body, black head and chest). She was mature, although she had yet to produce a litter. She came complete with cage and water tube wired to one side, straw, and a few food pellets. The older children were horrified to see her, my husband puzzled; I tried to be reasonable. Paulie begged and begged, promising to take full responsibility for the rat's care and feeding. In that moment of weakness all parents are guilty of, DeeDee was allowed to stay. The spot where her cage sat came to alternate between both kitchen and utility room.

I noticed right away—her habits.

After eating, that rat would tap her water tube with the upright palm of a forepaw, exactly the way a human would use a hand, then she would cup both forepaws to receive the water her tapping had released. She splashed that "handful" of water over her face and mouth and tapped some more, for enough water so that she could clean out each ear with an extended "finger."

I shook my head in disbelief the first time. But it wasn't long before I found myself studying her, especially when she seemed preoccupied with something else.

No doubt about it. DeeDee was an educated rat.

Maybe it was the sixth-grade classroom she had "graduated" from. I don't honestly know. All I know is, that rat was more human than animal. Always she would thoroughly clean herself after eating. And the way she used her forepaws, exactly like hands with fingers. You could think her name in your mind and she would perk up immediately and look at you. You could verbally converse with her and she would cock her head and listen. If you gave her a command, she would obey it. Change the words you used and she might have to think about her response, but she'd still respond—correctly.

She knew the difference between up and down, left and right, in and out, and she knew the name of each member of our family. Paulie said DeeDee had free run of the eraser tray under the blackboards along two walls of the classroom. Although DeeDee had behaved as a regular rat at school (except for her forays along the eraser tray), once in our home, she acted as if she had been trained by a professional animal trainer—in fact, better.

And you could converse with her. I mean you could carry on a fairly intelligent conversation, and the rat would respond appropriately . . . as if she understood every word. Not simple phrases like "Are you hungry?" but long sentences in multiple paragraphs. Naturally, it didn't take much time before all family members noticed DeeDee's unique temperament and her unusual intelligence. She became more than a pet. She became "family."

If one of us became ill, she would mope around and feign illness herself until that individual recovered. How she could pick up on such timing, I could never tell. She seemed to automatically "take on" anyone else's condition. After being bred several times and raising equally intelligent babies (she taught them all she knew), DeeDee became seriously ill and we put her to sleep so she would not suffer. With DeeDee gone, Paulie marched up to me one day and announced that DeeDee would come back. "Just wait and see," she said.

Several decades later, after my youngest daughter and I had moved from Idaho to the state of Virginia, and Paulie had given birth to her first child, she chanced upon a most unusual rat while absent-mindedly wandering through a shopping mall pet store. She bought the rat and brought it home with her. Her infant son immediately pointed to the rat and attempted to say the name "DeeDee." Paulie spun around and looked again, then called out, "DeeDee?" The rat jumped up and down, ran round and round, tapped her water tube, cupped her hands, splashed water over her face, and with long slender "fingers," cleaned out her ears. After such frenetic activity, the rat sat on her haunches, moved her nose closer to her cage wires, and Paulie swears . . . she smiled at her.

Paulie named her DeeDee II.

I went to visit one day. Nothing was said to me about my grandson's new pet. I spied the rat in her cage, and walked over for a closer look. The female was gray-hooded, instead of black as De Dee had been, so I thought nothing of it and turned to leave—when the rat started banging her cage and jumping up and down. I bent over and studied her. She reached out a paw to touch me. When our "fingers" met, a chill coursed through me. DeeDee! No doubt about it. The family's new pet was DeeDee come back.

Paulie grinned and the baby giggled.

I didn't know that animals could reincarnate, and with their same owners. DeeDee's return must have taken some doing, for we now live on the opposite side of the country from where we used to and my youngest daughter has become an adult. YET PAULIE'S BABY KNEW THE RAT, AND THE RAT KNEW THAT THE BABY WAS PAULIE'S!

I have no idea how this happened. I only know DeeDee, the educated rat, is back and she is just as clever and just as intelligent as ever.

It is true, at least as nearly as anyone can tell, that an animal can individualize once it shares life with a human—that is the "gift" we give our pets. But the extent to which an animal can be ensouled and evolve is still hotly debated, even in esoteric circles. As a researcher of the near-death experience and spiritual transformation, I can say this: animal pets are often there to greet those who cross over in death. The companionship we form with them *is* lasting.

Living Harmoniously with Wolves

According to Vincent Saviano of Mount Pleasant, South Carolina, the key to living harmoniously with a wolf is to give it the same attention that it would receive in a pack. Saviano became a part of the University of Minnesota wolf relocation project in 1980, and he acquired Bogart, a 130-pound timber wolf in 1988.

When Saviano and his wife Nancy have a drink after work, they see to it that Bogart has something to drink. When they nap, the black-white-and-brown wolf snuggles down for a snooze. When they greet visiting friends or family with an embrace and a kiss, Bogart stands up with his paws on their guests' shoulders and gives them a smooch of his own.

Saviano stresses the sociability of the wolf—as pack animals, they live in highly structured social units—and he loves to shatter the old "Red Riding Hood" fears of the forest creature as a scheming and dangerous villain.

According to Saviano, who has been a passionate advocate of wolves' rights since his student days at the University of California in the mid-1960s, wolves are shy, rather than agressive, animals.

Bogart has become an integral part of the Saviano family, gentle and loving as a child; and Vincent sees wolves as intelligent and beautiful creatures whose very existence on the planet has become endangered because of humankind. He feels that it is his mission to teach humans that they can learn to live side by side with wolves.

Canine Cupids, Bridesmaids and Groomsmen

For their August 1993 wedding, Mike Knecht and Tracy Hill of Red Deer, Alberta, Canada, saw to it that Mike's dog Bandit served as the best man.

All those in attendance agreed that Bandit was on his very best behavior and admirably performed all the duties of best man and best friend.

In July 1993, Margaret McDowell and David Cooper honeymooned in the hotel where their dogs had brought them together just a few months earlier.

Both Margaret and David were on week-long vacations with friends at a hotel in Devon, England, when David's dog Ike first got a good look at Margaret's dog Mara during a walk on the grounds.

The dogs' noses met, David chuckled later in retelling the story, and he and Margaret just happened to be on the other end of the leashes. Ike and Mara seemed to take an instant liking to one another, and so did David and Margaret.

After a brief conversation, the two vacationers went their separate ways and rejoined their friends, but David admitted to writer John Cooke that he couldn't get Margaret's lovely Irish voice out of his mind.

Margaret, of Belfast, Ireland, had likewise noted David's nice voice and the loving manner in which he treated his dog.

Margaret and David had to rely upon such verbal impressions, for they both happen to be blind.

When the two met again that night in the dining room, they began to talk in earnest and learned that they had an extrordinary number of things in common.

By the second night, they were holding hands. By the fourth night, David confessed that he had fallen in love and sincerely believed that they would end up married to one another.

Although smitten, Margaret felt that things were moving just a bit too fast for her.

After a tearful farewell, the two, both telephone operators, were soon calling each other daily from work and once again at home in the evening. After a few more weeks, David was flying to Belfast from his home in Worthing, England, for weekend visits.

A few more months of such long-distance romancing, and the two of them decided to get married and to honeymoon at the Devon hotel where they had met. Ike and Mara served as their escorts with resounding barks of approval.

Commenting on how close the two dogs had become, David suggested that they may have played Cupid as part of a very cunning plan. "Maybe they brought us together because *they* wanted to be together!"

Dog Serves as Dentist's Bridesmaid

When certain people say with great fervor that they consider their dog to be a member of the family, you can be assured that they mean it. A lovely bride in Glasgow, Scotland, even made her three-year-old mutt Sooky a member of her wedding party. The pooch was, in fact, one of the four bridesmaids.

When twenty-eight-year-old dentist Liz Wales prepared for her nuptials with Geoffrey Glass, she made no bones about the fact that Sooky, her beloved dog, would be an integral part of her wedding day. Well aware of Ms. Wales's genuine case of puppy love for her mixed-breed buddy, Glass wisely raised no objections to the inclusion of Ms. Sooky in the wedding party.

Sooky was even the guest of honor during the reception and was seated in a special place at the bridal table.

"Sooky is one of the family," the new Mrs. Glass said. "Since this was my special day, I definitely wanted her to be part of it."

Charm, the Newfoundland Matchmaker

Kimberly Pearce of Mason City, Iowa, trusts her dogs' instincts on just about everything. "They're always right," she told us. Her Newfoundland dogs, Charm and Fisher, are certified search and rescue dogs.

Kim frequently gets calls from police departments requesting the assistance of her gentle giant canine friends. Their mission is usually to locate missing people or to hunt down escaped convicts.

Even in temperatures of fifty degrees below zero, Kim and her dogs have braved the weather to be of service. Newfoundlands have the amazing ability to smell a human scent even under fifty feet of snow! The longest search Charm and Fisher have been on so far is fourteen hours in subzero temperatures, Kim told us.

Kim says, even in circumstances when she was told that her dogs were on the wrong trail according to the police, her dogs turned out to be right! Five other teams of dogs had already gone down the one trail her dogs were heading, and they came up with nothing. Obeying the police, Kim called her dogs in the other direction.

After coming up with nothing further on that trail either, Kim stood her ground that she was going to follow her dogs' lead. In going back where they wanted to go first—they had been right. Unfortunately, the missing person they were seeking was not alive, but the body was found there.

Especially after that experience of witnessing her dogs' accuracy, Kim told us:

"If there's one thing I have to work on—I'm convinced it is to learn to trust my dogs *even more* than I already do.

"In search and rescue missions it is essential to know how to 'read' your dog," Kim continued. "Whether a pet or a rescue dog—it's similar. Since our pets don't talk, it's important to establish a bond with your pet. That special connection will help you understand each other. In place of speech, dogs have a much keener sense of smell and hearing than we do, so of course they rely heavily on those senses for communicating."

We know this from working with our own dog, Moses.

Dogs might be attempting to "tell" us something that doesn't make sense to us until we learn to trust them and pay attention to their cues. Soon they will make sense to us and then new cues can be added, then you're communicating! Some cues our pets might use to talk to us or tell us what they want or how they feel are often misinterpreted, because until we try to think in a different way—from their perspective—it wouldn't make sense to us.

Kim told us a story that illustrates the point perfectly.

On one occasion she had to be out of town for four days. Even though her pet was staying with Kim's mother, the dog refused to eat anything at all and was moping around and acting depressed. The dog went from room to room, looking for Kim. Not finding her, it frantically went everywhere again—apparently just attempting to find anything that smelled like Kim.

All that could be found was one dirty sock, which, for some reason, was in the bottom of an old laundry basket. The dog carried that sock everywhere, even sleeping with it. For the entire four days that's all the dog did—mope and snuggle the sock—occasionally looking out the window.

When Kim returned, her pet abandoned the sock and "returned to happy" . . . then had a huge meal!

It would have been normal for Kim's mom to grab the sock away and put it up, perhaps not even making the connection that it was her daughter's sock and a comforter to the lonely pup. Understanding what was being communicated, Kim's mom just kept reassuring the pet that Kimmy would be back soon and everything would be all right.

Kim might have to add "matchmaker" to the list of accomplishments and capabilities of her search and rescue dogs. Charm seemed intent on being extra hospitable and affectionate to one of the guys that Kimberly dated. "Charm knew he was for me," Kim told us. Charm was intent on gently taking Scott's hand into her mouth and pulling him into the living room—as if to say "come on in, this is where you belong!"

"Never before has Charm done that except to me. That's a very loving and playful way of telling me how happy to see me she is! As soon as I saw Charm 'take Scott by the hand'—I *knew* he was the one!"

People Who Prefer Pets to Their Human Mates

A poll conducted by the *National Enquirer* in 1994 revealed the somewhat shocking statistics that three out of four people talk more to their pets than to their spouse or sweetheart.

Enquirer reporter John Blosser said that they queried one hundred men and one hundred women in Los Angeles, Denver, Dallas, Orlando, and Boston. "Do you talk more with your pet than you do your partner?" And an astounding 73 percent answered *yes.*

Blosser stated that there was almost no difference between the sexes, with 74 percent of men and 72 percent of women admitting that they more often talk things over with pooch or pussycat.

A thirty-year-old Boston physician named Elizabeth told pollsters that she had three cats and that she probably talked "more to them than to anyone, including my husband. I can tell them my troubles and they'll listen for hours—so long as I keep scratching their heads."

A company vice president in Los Angeles said that his sheepdog agreed with everything he said—and this wasn't the case with his wife!

Although we have presented dozens of cases of human/pet interaction in the pages of this book, we do not advocate forming such tight relationships with your pet that you exclude the company of humans. Your loving pet needs to be recognized and respected as a loving member of a companion species and prized for his or her own unique contributions to your life. Our pets are not surrogate humans. They are sovereign entities in their own right, and they touch our hearts in their own special ways.

A Pet's Devotion Extends Beyond the Grave

In his March 5, 1993, column in the *Quad City Times*, Bill Wundram provides the background story on the finely crafted, life-sized granite dog that serves as a grave marker in the Rock Island, Illinois, Chippiannock Cemetery.

According to cemetery manager Greg Vogele, the statue is a replica of a devoted Newfoundland, who is said to have died of a broken heart over the deaths of two children buried beside the life-sized marker. In 1878 an epidemic of diphtheria struck the area, particularly focusing its deadly attacks upon children. According to old newspaper accounts, the lung disease brought a swift death. One day little five-year-old Eddie Dimick and his sister Josie, eight, were in school—and two days later they were dead.

The faithful Newfoundland, who had daily accompanied them to school and waited nearby to walk them home at the end of the day, was completely distraught by the deaths of his little master and mistress. He walked behind the hearse that carried the little caskets to the cemetery and returned daily to grieve at their graves.

After a time, the family noticed that the faithful dog had assumed the same pattern with the memory of the children that he had maintained during their lives. He would walk to the cemetery each morning and lie on their gravesite until dark.

In less than a year after the deaths of Eddie and Josie, the big dog, who had regularly refused food, literally died of sorrow for his little human charges. He was buried on the family acreage.

The children's father, O.J. Dimick, a local entrepreneur of considerable wealth, had been so touched by the dog's devotion that he commissioned a Chicago sculptor to create a life-sized replica of the Newfoundland that could be placed over the graves of Eddie and Josie. Contemporary accounts in the possession of historian Kim Bolyard record Dimick's specifications that the dog's likeness be "first class, with the animal's head resting on its paws, a natural position." Other accounts allude to Dimick's wish that the "noble brute" should forever watch over the two little ones whose image he so revered.

Mrs. Bolyard said that her research is still attempting to seek out the faithful Newfoundland's identity, for she would like to place a little marker beside the statue identifying the devoted dog by name.

The pet dog of William the Silent, ruler of the Netherlands, became so despondent after the assassination of his master in 1584 that he would not eat or drink—and he soon followed him in death.

Diana Visited Her Master's Grave Every Day for Seventeen Months

When Mario Allegritti died in February 1989, his faithful dog Diana ran away.

Mrs. Ida Allegritti of Citivella Roveto, Italy, knew that the mongrel dog had been devoted to her husband—Diana had even attended his funeral—so she assumed that the pooch had decided to leave the hearth now that Mario was dead. Her sons had searched for Diana off and on for a few days, then reached the same conclusion: She had gone off to search for greener pastures.

Fourteen months later, as Mrs. Allegritti stopped by the cemetery to visit her husband's grave, she was surprised to see the caretaker trying to chase a dog away from the tombstone.

"I'm sorry," he apologized. "But this stray mongrel comes here every night. I have tried my best to get rid of it."

Mrs. Allegritti was astonished to see that the dog in question was the disappearing Diana. "That's my husband's dog!" she shouted at the caretaker. "Leave her alone."

The widow tried to pick the dog up in her arms, but Diana wriggled free and began to whine. Once unrestrained, she went directly to Mario's tombstone and kissed his picture, which had been set in a cameo over the grave.

After that little ritual had been performed, Diana seemed willing to accompany Mrs. Allegritti to her car. Once back in familiar surroundings, the dog seemed happy and contented to be home.

But the next morning Diana had once again disappeared, and Mrs. Allegritti was certain that she would return to her husband's grave that evening.

The widow's guess was correct. That night while she watched, Diana entered the cemetery, walked directly to Mario's tombstone, licked his picture, then crouched in front of the grave, not once taking her eyes from her master's likeness.

From that evening on, either Mrs. Allegritti or one of her sons accompanies Diana to the cemetery to visit Mario's grave. On each occasion, Diana licks her master's picture, then lies motionless in front of the tombstone.

In 1991, the members of the San Rocco Award jury in Camoglio, Italy, awarded Diana the "Most Loyal Dog of the Year" prize.

Faithful Shep Waited at the Railroad Station Six Years for His Master to Return

Old Ray Castles, a sheepherder, didn't feel very well when he came to town in Fort Benton, Montana, one day in 1936. His loyal collie-German shepherd mix, Shep, knew something was wrong when Ray went into the hospital, but he just curled his tail around himself and sat down to wait it out.

A few days later, when they took his master out of the place in a wooden box, Shep was really getting confused. The two of them had become inseparable companions out there alone with the sheep herds, night after night, month after month. Now Ray didn't pet him, didn't speak to him. He was stone cold and in a box.

Some men loaded Ray-in-the-box aboard a Great Northern train headed east, and Shep was left all alone, whining and confused. The husky dog seemed to understand about trains. Some folks got on while others got off. Perhaps Ray would be back the next day.

In those days, Fort Benton received four daily incoming trains. Shep was there the next day to meet all four.

When Ray didn't step off any of them, Shep came back the next day. And the next. And the next.

The faithful Shep maintained his mournful vigil for nearly six years, greeting each train with expectation, then walking dejectedly away from each disappointment.

Eventually the collie-German shep dug himself a kind of home under the station's boardwalk so he wouldn't have to walk so far back and forth to check on the train arrivals. The railroad workers didn't run him off. In fact, they developed a healthy respect for such a remarkable display of faithfulness and loyalty, and most of them saw to it that old Shep got plenty of scraps to munch on. Some of the workers even brought him old blankets to help keep him warm in the cold of winter.

In 1942, at the age of fifteen, Shep slipped under the wheels of one of the trains that he came running to meet and his six-year-vigil came to an end. When some railroad workers buried the old dog on the top of a bluff overlooking the tracks, one of them was heard to remark that Shep and Ray were finally together once again. Later, some railroad employees erected a monument in loving memory of a dog's incredible devotion to his master.

In 1992, fifty years after Shep's death, the people of Fort Benton held a grand ceremony at Shep's monument. Eighty-year-old Joel Overholser, who still worked at the Fort Benton *River Press*, remembered old Shep well. "His name has become a byword for loyalty and devotion," he said.

Devoted Dog Stands Vigil Over Dead Master's Body for Three Months

When the collie was found, he was so weak from hunger that he couldn't even stand. But the loyal dog had completed his vigil. He had stood guard over his dead master's body for nearly three months.

Police Constable Martin Coups told journalists that searchers had found Ruswarp, the fourteen-year-old collie-mix, lying barely conscious beside the body of Graham Nuttall, forty-one, who had apparently suffered a heart attack while hiking the frost-covered hills of central Wales in January 1990. Although the dog may have left the body of his master long enough to hunt down small game, it was believed that Ruswarp had lived primarily off his own body fat and water from the spring where his master had died.

Nuttall, a bachelor and a devoted railroading enthusiast, had named his faithful canine companion after a train depot in North Yorkshire.

Police Constable Coups said that his heart had gone out to the dog who was too feeble to stand, let alone walk, so he carried him five miles to an inn. Fearful that Ruswarp would die in his arms, the officer gave him some chocolate candy—which he wolfed right down.

Ruswarp was taken to a veterinary clinic in Llandrindod Wells, where accomplished veterinarians treated him for anemia and malnutrition.

Although he had been in a pitiful, confused condition when he was brought to the clinic, Ruswarp soon rallied and became something of a regional hero. Everyone was quick to note that loyal friends such as Ruswarp are hard to find.

The Dog that Brought His Master Back from the Grave

And how about a dog's quick thinking that enabled his master quite literally to return to life from the grave?

In 1643, John Granville of Kirkhampton, England, was a sixteen-year-old soldier who fought in the Battle of Newbury. Wounded and left for dead, he was buried on the field of battle—then dug up by his faithful dog, who refused to let his master die.

It was certainly a propitious occurrence for Granville that his dog brought him back from the dead, for he had the good fortune to live another fifty-seven years.

Sheltering You and Your Pet in the Golden Pyramid of Love

We are certain that, if you are a sensitive pet owner, you have noticed that your pet gives you nonjudgmental, unconditional love. While such a state is very difficult for us humans to attain in our world of taxes, tears and strife, once we can—if even briefly—achieve a degree of unconditional love in our hearts, we soon discover that such an energy is not easily depleted. If we can learn to fill ourselves with love, it becomes so much more difficult to express hatred, envy, jealousy or greed. It is so much more difficult for negativity to touch us when we are filled with love.

When you are filled with love, you find that you cannot hold it within your being. You must pour it forth upon others or it will stagnate.

If you try to bottle up love within you, you will find that it simply cannot keep. It will soon sour. Love must be given away to others so that you may receive it afresh.

Even now as you read these words, begin to feel unconditional love for your pet pouring into your body. Even now, begin to feel the same kind of nonjudgmental love for your pet as he or she feels toward you.

Feel this love entering you through the very top of your head and moving down your body to fill up your entire physical vessel.

Be aware of it filling your feet, your ankles, your legs, your hips, your stomach, chest, and back.

Feel it entering your arms. Sense it moving up your spine. Know that it has entered your neck, your shoulders, your head. Understand that you are now filled with love to the top of your head. Be aware that you are vibrating, glowing, with unconditional love.

Now imagine that directly above your head is a beautiful golden pyramid, a pyramid of love. Understand that this golden pyramid contains vibrations of unconditional love from the Creator Spirit. Be aware that these vibrations of unconditional love emanate from the pyramid and enter the top of your head, then move down to the area around your heart.

Now visualize your pet. Visualize a golden beam of light from your heart streaking across the space between you to touch your beloved pet in its heart. Feel strongly the link-up that you have achieved with your pet.

Now imagine that together you and your pet are sending your combined love around the earth. Visualize that you will touch the hearts of animals that are feeling unloved, mistreated, abused. See you and your pet with your combined energy of love reaching out, and make contact with all those animals who feel unloved and unwanted. Visualize that their newfound love joins that love-energy of you and your pet and that you begin to send this powerful new vibration of unconditional love around the planet.

Feel you and your pet pouring out unconditional love from your hearts. See your light of love streaming out all over the earth. Know that it is touching the hearts of lonely, despondent, angry people . . . people who do not know love . . . people who abuse animals and mistreat pets. Be aware that your love is reaching those people who pollute the environment, who needlessly slaughter sea life and wildlife throughout the planet. See your love easing their bitterness of spirit. Feel your love helping to raise their consciousness. Be aware that your love is aiding them in the balancing of their energies.

Be aware that you and your pet are giving and receiving anew the unconditional love vibration. Feel a new, dynamic burst of the energy, the strength, the God-vibration within the frequency of love that surrounds you. Know that the more love you pour forth from your heart, the more love from the God-Source you will receive from the golden pyramid of love above your head. The more love you transmit, the more you will be energized.

Visualize the unconditional love you and your pet have sent around the world coming back to the golden pyramid above your head. See that it has grown and has strength and vitality. Be aware that, because you have given love, you have received even greater amounts of love energy in return.

Practice this broadcasting of the love vibration from the golden pyramid on a regular basis, and you will will see a marked improvement in your loving relationship with your pet. You will be aware of a greater mutual respect and admiration growing between you. At the same time, you will achieve a higher level of respect for all animal and human life and you will be more attuned to the spark of the Divine that exists within all of God's creatures, great and small.

As you become more sensitive to the true spiritual balance of the planet and all of the lifeforms upon its surface, waters and skies, you will feel more a part of the energy that connects you with the power of love that binds you with your pet in the Oneness of all life.